PENGUIN BOOKS
INVESTONOMY

Dearly known as PK by his loving patrons and supporters, Pranjal Kamra is the Founder and CEO of Finology Ventures Pvt. Ltd. He has one core mission—to make financial education and investing accessible and 'super simple' for the common man. And his bootstrapped start-up has certainly been meeting the expectations.

Ardently committed to his purpose, Pranjal has created the largest space for prolific financial education through his YouTube Channel, which has over 3 million subscribers, and Finology, which boasts over 7 lakh dedicated patrons. An element that offered his talents the right boost was his education at the National Institute of Securities Market and Hidayatullah National Law University.

This book gives a glimpse into his simplified view of the world of finance and is certain to enlighten the reader effortlessly.

To know more about him and Finology, visit www.finology.in.

INVESTONOMY

THE STOCK MARKET GUIDE THAT MAKES YOU RICH

PRANJAL KAMRA

PENGUIN BOOKS

An imprint of Penguin Random House

PENGUIN BOOKS

USA | Canada | UK | Ireland | Australia
New Zealand | India | South Africa | China

Penguin Books is part of the Penguin Random House group of companies
whose addresses can be found at global.penguinrandomhouse.com

Published by Penguin Random House India Pvt. Ltd
4th Floor, Capital Tower 1, MG Road,
Gurugram 122 002, Haryana, India

First published in Penguin Books by Penguin Random House India 2022

Copyright © Pranjal Kamra 2022

10 9 8 7 6 5 4 3 2 1

The views and opinions expressed in this book are the authors' own and the
facts are as reported by them which have been verified to the extent possible,
and the publishers are not in any way liable for the same.

ISBN 9780143455042

Typeset in Adobe Caslon Pro by Manipal Technologies Limited, Manipal

www.penguin.co.in

To the readers:
'This book is a roadmap to convert your love–hate relationship with the stock market into an unshakeable bond.'

Contents

Preface

Innocent lay investors have all the rights to earn big from the stock market.

This book aims to provide them with the required fundamental knowledge. But that's not all! If you've already got your hands dirty in equity investing, this book will help you expand the horizon of your knowledge.

Investonomy has been written to educate investors about the fundamental rules of stock investment. The book also reveals basic strategies and rules that an investor must keep in mind while picking up stocks. A thorough reading of this book will ensure that the reader is fully educated about how to invest in stocks successfully.

The book also busts popular myths like:

- To be a successful stock investor, you need to be a statistician, mathematician, or financial guru.
- The stock market is like gambling in a casino.

- Stock analysis is challenging to learn, and seeking professional help is a must.

Why is *Investonomy* relevant to you?

I'm guessing that you wish to get rich sometime in life. I mean, who doesn't have the desire to be immensely rich? If that's not you, please develop an urge to earn big and then continue reading!

Now, when you search for available options to quench your thirst for 'big, rewarding returns', you end up gambling money in stocks (like many people around you). While your money is on the line, you're illogically hopeful that you will get a positive return. But unfortunately, the market doesn't move accordingly, and you lose your hard-earned money. This leaves you heartbroken, and you lose trust in stock market investing!

But then, just one anecdote shared by a friend about how he made significant profits from stocks rekindles your lost desire of investing in stocks! So, with rejuvenated hope, you make a few more attempts and again start losing. How do you feel at this point? Betrayed? Frustrated? Lost?

Knowing well the pain areas of stock investment, the thought of penning a book crossed my mind to help every potential investor who rightly thinks that stock investments can help them get rich. My sole purpose in writing this book is to empower individual investors who have never tried investing in stocks or have been unsuccessful in their attempts.

Investonomy aims to give you the means to make substantial money from the stock market with the right intent of investment. The book is a roadmap for fuelling your ambitions and chasing your passion.

Pranjal Kamra
CEO, Finology Ventures Pvt. Ltd
(A SEBI-registered Investment Advisory firm)

My Inspiration to Write This Book!

I had come across many incidents that broke my heart when I learnt how innocent investors in the stock market are fooled into losing all their hard-earned savings. Without wasting much of your time, I would like to mention two such incidents:

One of the victims of stock fraudulence was a young professional from Bengaluru who was duped by a stock broking company, Deceptive Brokers Pvt. Ltd (name changed on purpose). The company claimed to be a reputed stockbroking firm and shared a plan which required an investment value of Rs 40,000. As per the firm, the investment would double in value in just a few months.

Finding the deal lucrative, the victim agreed to invest in it. But soon, the company pulled the innocent victim into a bigger trap by encouraging him to invest further, stating that the market was up-and-coming and could fetch him more significant returns. The poor young investor was genuinely unaware of the fraudulent activities carried out openly in this industry. He ended up investing up to Rs 4 lakh, all with the hope of increasing his investment value.

Another sad story was that of a retired senior citizen who was approached by a stock brokerage firm. The firm promised him that by making small investments into stocks, he would be able to grow his pension money. The victim thought that with an increased income, he would live with the utmost comfort in his old age, so he invested in one of the schemes.

As per the policy, the company would invest 20 per cent of his pension money every month to turn it into promising returns. After two months, when the investor asked the firm to confirm the proofs of the investments done till date, the firm came up with explanations of all sorts but didn't provide any actual evidence! The poor victim insisted that the firm return his money, but all his efforts went in vain.

Both these incidents created a spark in me to share my first-hand knowledge of stock investment for the sake of retail investors, who fall prey to lucrative deals offered by the so-called stock advisory firms. In this quest to help innocent people, I ended up writing this book.

I want to extend my heartfelt thanks to you for giving your valuable time to this book. I dedicate this book to my family, who inspired me and supported me in my journey of discovering my passion for stock market investment.

Disclaimer

The author is an investor and a regular participant in the stock markets and consequently may have held or may be holding positions in some stocks mentioned in the books. The content, including the formulae, concepts, examples, charts, and graphs in this book, has been taken from third-party resources. We have tried to express ourselves in this book as precisely and accurately as we could, and any errors, if found, are entirely accidental and not intentional. While we have taken care to update the information to the extent possible, up till current date, we would like to remind our readers that figures change every quarter. Before using any information, the readers must use correct data from authentic and trustworthy resources. This book contains an honest, unbiased approach to stock investment and has been written with the sole purpose of benefiting you. However, the book, its title, and the contents of the same do not promise any gains to the reader. Each reader is recommended to do their own research and seek appropriate advice before making any investments.

Stocks/data/analyses/pictorial representations and graphs used in this book are illustrative and for informative purposes and our readers' pleasure only. They should not be taken as recommendations from the author or be construed as legal, tax, investment, financial, or other advice. Nothing mentioned in this book constitutes a solicitation, recommendation, endorsement, or offer by the author or the publisher to buy or sell any securities or other financial instruments in Indian or any other jurisdiction.

The author does not guarantee the accuracy, adequacy, or completeness of any information provided in this book and is not responsible for any errors or omissions or for the results obtained from the use of such information. Neither the publisher nor the author has any financial liability whatsoever to any user on account of the use of the information provided.

One sincere piece of advice to our readers is to research thoroughly before investing, as money does not grow on trees. And we, as writers, must not be held responsible for any losses incurred by investing in stocks using the information shared here. Our readers alone assume the sole responsibility of evaluating the merits and risks associated with the use of any information or other contents in the book. We shall not be held liable for any losses or damages incurred by our readers under any circumstance. We recommend consulting appropriate financial advisors prior to making any investment.

Lastly, many examples used by the author, including names, characters, places, and incidents, are either the product of the author's imagination or fictitiously used. Any resemblance to actual persons, living or dead, businesses, companies, events, or locales is entirely coincidental.

The Best Accident
That Happened in My Life

Investing

I'm sharing this story with you just to make you think that when an inexperienced guy like me, with no background in share investment, can make it big, then why can't you?

A few years ago, my father gifted me a TVS Wego on my birthday. But even better, he also gave me Rs 20,000 to invest in shares. Being a novice, I took an emotional decision and purchased the stock of TVS Motors with it. Bingo! I was lucky to have made good money out of this transaction, and I got a nice kick out of it! I then started investing more in stocks, and my investing journey began.

After tasting success in the first shot, I became overconfident and thought that I had mastered the art of investing. However, my luck did not favour me in my next two purchases. I bought stocks worth Rs 200 and Rs 30 each. The current value of these stocks today is Re 0 and Rs 3,

respectively. As I look back, I realize that my success with TVS Motors was nothing but mere beginner's luck.

By the way, do you know that one who claims to have never lost money in stock trading is either lying or has never invested? Only if you lose will you learn.

Back in 2015, I was a struggling law student, and my father believed that a law degree alone would not be enough for a promising career. So, he enrolled me in the Company Secretary course. One day, along with dozens of emails that the CS institute used to send me, I got an email informing me about an institute called NISM.

When I first heard about the National Institute of Securities Markets (NISM), I was thrilled to know that an institute existed that was solely dedicated to the securities market. So, I went ahead and pursued a one-year certificate course from NISM on stock investment.

After struggling for half a decade in figuring out my calling, I finally felt that I belonged to this place. I loved reading about value investing and fundamental analysis to such an extent that I would immerse myself in reading day in and day out.

My constant perseverance to discover more about the stock market made me a continuous learner. Soon, I started a YouTube channel on the stock market and mutual fund investment. After a year of starting the channel, which goes by the name Pranjal Kamra, I incorporated my company, Finology Ventures Pvt. Ltd, which is the first SEBI-registered Investment Advisory Company in Chhattisgarh.

1

The Stock Market Is the Gateway to Dreaming Big!

You must have often heard a friend say, 'I wish I had enough money to open up a garment business,' or 'I wish I had money to start my restaurant.' On hearing such ambitions, I often applaud my friends and say, 'Great, go ahead, chase your dreams.' But there is something that stops them from chasing their dreams.

So, what is that *something* that stops them from dreaming big?

1. It could be a *lack of knowledge, experience, and skills.*
2. It could be a *lack of funds or sourcing.*
3. It could be a *lack of time and support.*

Or it could be all three of these, put together and stopping them from chasing their dreams. But do we really need these three factors to build a business, or is there a way around them? Think hard!

What if I tell you that you can become the owner of a business without knowing how to run it? What if I tell you that you can still own businesses without funds or sourcing? What if I tell you that you can own businesses without giving your time and support? Sounds unrealistic, doesn't it?

It is a fact that these are only possible in the opportunity-filled world of stock investment.

What Can You Expect from the Stock Market?

The stock market comes with multiple opportunities to grow your wealth. Here are a few things that it offers you.

- Investing in the stock market is a great way to own good businesses, as your money is in the hands of fully dedicated business managers. You invest your money in promising ventures, run and managed by highly competent, proactive thinkers like Warren Buffett, Ratan Tata, Adi Godrej, etc. These people work each day to create synergies with a large team of professionals only to make their businesses succeed. When their businesses grow, your money grows. So do you think you would ever find a better deal to grow your money, than legends like Mr Ratan Tata and Mr Adi Godrej managing it for you?
- You can invest a small amount of money in businesses. This money multiplies enormously over time due to increased business value. You have the freedom to invest as low as Rs 500.
- You can just invest your money and forget about it. It is the best way to let your money grow in the stock market, as businesses take time to grow.

So, can we be assured that stock investment paints such an ideal picture? Not really! It requires a great deal of patience as an investor.

Just think: Does a newly established business earn you profit right from the first day? No, right? We patiently wait for our businesses to grow; we work 12 hours a day for years together to earn profit from our businesses. Stock investment is the same; you need to pick the right stocks and give them time to grow. The value of stocks increases in the long run when the business grows, and it takes time to achieve that.

So, before beginning this enticing journey of stock investment, let's try to answer a few questions to test your current understanding of the stock market. Don't worry if you don't know some or all of these answers. Just take some wild guesses instead.

Please answer the following questions quickly and instinctively.

1. Can you get assured returns from stocks?
   a. Yes
   b. No

2. Do you need to analyse financial and technical charts to be a successful stock investor?
   a. Yes
   b. No

3. Which of the following can bring you the highest returns?
   a. Land
   b. Gold
   c. Stocks
   d. Debentures
   e. Fixed deposits

4. Can you easily learn and practice stock investment?
    a. Yes
    b. No

5. Can you become richer than you ever dreamt of by investing in stocks?
    a. Yes, possibly
    b. No, never

6. Should you still be investing in stocks if you are rich enough?
    a. Yes
    b. No

7. Out of 132 crore people in India, how many invest in the stock market?
    a. Only 10 per cent
    b. Only 20 per cent
    c. About 40 per cent
    d. Only 2 per cent

8. Despite India being one of the most populous countries, why do most Indians not invest in stocks?
    a. They are unaware of investing rules
    b. They are scared of losing money
    c. They quit because they have lost money
    d. All of the above

Don't worry if you got some answers wrong. The following chapters will be eye-openers as you discover this wonderful, mesmerizing world of stocks. So, hold on tight as we begin to dig deeper into stock investment. I wish you a happy and fulfilling reading.

The answers to the above questions are:

1. No; 2. No; 3. C; 4. Yes; 5. Yes, possibly; 6. Yes; 7. Only 2%; 8. All of the above.

2

Do You Wish to Have Complete Financial Independence?

Caught in a rat race of working tirelessly to make ends meet, we often wonder whether we can ever have it all without being trapped in such a menace.

Or, say, do you often dream of becoming financially independent by the time you turn 40? Or do you wish to own riches large enough so that you don't have to restrict your expenses anymore? Or do you wish to take a few moments off and enjoy life while your bank balance still rises?

If yes, then this chapter will excite you.

Introspection

Let us dig a little deeper and see how well you understand your financial needs. Here is a worksheet that you need to answer quickly.

How to Use the Worksheet

- Given below are some questions.
- Each question has four options to choose from, with marks allotted.

The following questions will help you understand how much money you will be able to make five years down the line. I request you to take a pencil and quickly mark down the answers.

1. What is your aim behind investing money?

Options	Points
a. You want to accumulate wealth	4
b. You want to buy a house	3
c. You want to do your retirement planning	2
d. You want to provide for your child's education or marriage	1

Your answer _____

2. When will you withdraw the invested money in the future?

Options	Points
a. After 10 years	4
b. In 5–10 years	3
c. In 2–5 years	2
d. Within 2 years	1

3. Are you the only breadwinner of the family?

Options	Points
a. No	4
b. Yes, with one dependent	3
c. I have two to four dependents	2
d. I have more than four dependents	1

4. Do you have any financial obligations like loan repayment?

Options	Points
a. No	4
b. Yes, less than 10 per cent of my earnings are utilized in EMIs	3
c. Yes, 10–20 per cent of my earnings are utilized in EMIs	2
d. Yes, more than 20 per cent of my earnings are utilized in EMIs	1

5. Which of the following investment returns are you looking at? (The following table shows the range of Compound Annual Growth Rate or CAGR you can achieve by choosing the respective options.)

Options	Best Case	Worst Case	Average Return	Points
a.	50%	- 28%	12%	4
b.	30%	- 15%	10%	3
c.	15%	- 5%	9%	2
d.	7%	0%	7%	1

6. If you are offered a promising job, what compensation structure will you choose?

Options		Points
a.	Employee stock options with a current value of Rs 1,00,000 and prospects for further appreciation	4
b.	An upfront bonus of Rs 1,00,000	3
c.	A 10 per cent pay increase in your salary of Rs 4,00,000	2
d.	A 3-year job guarantee	1

Marking Scheme

Calculate the total marks based on the options you chose.

Total Marks	Category	Percentage of Allocation			
		Equity Large-Cap	Equity Mid-Cap and Multi-Cap	Fixed Deposits	Gold
21–24	Aggressive	25	60	10	5
16–20	Moderately Aggressive	30	50	10	10
11–15	Moderate	40	20	20	20
6–10	Conservative	20	0	70	10

So, now you know what kinds of risks and returns you are ready to take as an investor. You are also aware of how much money you will make in the near future with your current choice of financial investments. The exercise we did also revealed your earning potential if you invest in the stock market.

This awareness is the first step in creating riches bigger than you have ever dreamt of. Well done! You have analysed and understood what, in my opinion, 70 per cent of people fail to understand about their own finances. And let me tell you that *a good beginning is half the journey.*

3

The Basics of Stock Market Investment

In the words of the famous value investor Peter Lynch, 'Everyone has the brainpower to follow the stock market. If you made it through fifth-grade math, you can do it.'

What Is a Share?

A company needs capital or funding to grow, expand, and function. The popular way of generating money is to take a loan from the bank, on which you pay a fixed interest every month. Another way of generating funds is by releasing shares of the company that are bought by the public.

A company's capital is divided into smaller units called shares. A 'share' is a term used to describe a part of the ownership of a company. If you own a share of the company, you hold a part of the company's ownership. Thus, you are entitled to receive your share of the earnings of that company.

When investors buy shares and become part-owners of a company, they are entitled to a percentage of the company's profit, and their liability is only limited to the share value. The benefit is that despite the investors being owners of the company, they do not bear the losses beyond their investment value. The other advantage is that due to the presence of a stock exchange, they can quickly sell or buy shares of any other company at any time they want.

Let's look at an example. Infosys is the brainchild of N.R. Narayana Murthy, Nandan Nilekani, and others who have been the key drivers of the business for three decades. When Infosys was incorporated in 1981, it wasn't making big money even though it was doing reasonably well.

In 1993, Infosys went public. It released its shares, but who would invest in a company with no labour, no machinery, and no factories? Only a handful of investors invested merely Rs 10,000 in Infosys stock, and today, they're all multi-millionaires!

The rest is history. Infosys quickly rose to become at par with the Tatas. Today, Nandan Nilekani's worth is more than Rs 3,000 crore!

This is how, by releasing shares, a company borrows money from the public. The money is borrowed in exchange for ownership of the company. So when the company grows, the share prices soar, bringing profits to the shareholders.

What Defines a Stock Market?

If you're a smart shopper, you'll enjoy exploring and shopping in the stock market. And, if you're not a smart shopper, you'll soon become one in the stock market. I say this because the stock market facilitates stock trading, i.e., both buying and selling of stocks. In a typical marketplace, you'll just buy, but here you'll sell as well; you control both aspects, and thereby your fate is in your own hands.

Two Essential Components of the Stock Market

The two important participants in the stock market are:

1. **Investors:** Investors engage in a low-risk game that involves fundamental analysis of a company before investing.
2. **Speculators:** Speculators are involved in high-risk betting on the expected price movement of listed securities.

The basic differences between Investing and Speculating

S. No.	Basis of Differentiation	Investing	Speculating
1.	Aim of investment	Invest money safely by applying the fundamental analysis of stock valuation.	Bet money on stocks to gain good profit.
2.	Basis of investment	Based on the fundamental value analysis of the company	Based on market rumours and stock price changes
3.	The duration	Long term	Short term
4.	The risk involved	Moderate to low risk	High risk

S. No.	Basis of Differentiation	Investing	Speculating
5.	Returns on investment	The benefit comes when the value of the business increases.	The profit comes when the prices of the shares move as expected.
6.	Expectations	The expected rate of return is modest and realistic.	The expected rate of return is high and unrealistic at times.
7.	Source of money	An investor invests his own money.	A speculator borrows money and invests in stocks.
8.	Pattern of earning	Returns may be delayed, but the source of income is stable.	Erratic source of income and may involve losses as well.
9.	Approach to investment	The investor takes a well-thought-out decision after analysing the value of the company.	The speculator is instinctive and looks at making immediate gains.
10.	Investor's psychology	An investor looks at the underlying ethics, values, and fundamentals before investing.	A speculator is desperate to earn money, and that's the key driver to buy stocks.
11.	Success probability	The probability of losing money is lower, as the decision is backed by in-depth analysis.	The probability of losing money is 50 per cent, as speculating is similar to betting.

Though the investors bring a lot of stability into the market, speculators are also equally crucial for creating a balance. They play two critical roles:

- *Speculators bring fluctuations in the pricing of stocks.* The volatility gives investors a fair chance to buy shares at low prices.
- *Speculators trade stocks frequently, which makes the volumes of shares for buying and selling available.*

The Significance of the Stock Market

A stock exchange, commonly referred to as a stock market, is a platform where buyers and sellers of shares come together to trade stocks.

Other important functions of the stock market are as follows:

1. *Price discovery:* The stock market enables the fair valuation of stock pricing by providing a transparent medium. The shares are priced and evaluated based on their demand and supply. If a company is expected to perform well, the demand for its share rises, and hence, the price goes up.
2. *Liquidity:* The stock market provides you a 24×7 opportunity to sell or buy stocks as and when you desire. This ensures easy liquidity, bringing in a great deal of convenience to you as an investor.
3. *The habit of saving and investment:* As you can invest even a small amount of money in the stock market, it enhances the practice of savings among the people.

4. *Expansion of business:* Any listed company can quickly meet the need for funds required to expand its business.
5. *Provides opportunities for speculation:* To ensure liquidity, the stock exchange provides an opportunity for healthy speculation to its investors.

The stock exchange is necessary for the economic growth of the country. By trading shares, corporates can build a financial corpus and use it to expand their operations or deploy the capital raised for the company's benefit. It should not be viewed as a place to gamble or trade; instead, it is a place to invest and let your money grow.

How Do You Make Money as a Shareholder?

When you hold a share of the company, there are mainly two types of income you can earn. One is the dividend income, and the other is the increase in the value of your investment. Let's understand each of these.

*   *Dividend income:* The profits earned by a company are either reinvested in the business or given away to its shareholders. The part of the profits that is given to shareholders is called a dividend.
*   *Appreciation of the value of investment:* One of the primary reasons to invest money in the market is to see the value of the investment appreciate. The demand for the share is affected by the company's performance, resulting in stock price fluctuations. And the value of the investment appreciates when the price of the share increases.

These were the absolute basics of stock market investment, written to give you a clear picture of how shares work. This knowledge will act as a foundation for the rest of the chapters.

Let me tell you that even though the stock market is highly talked about and written about, most people are unaware of its fundamental realities. Those who wish to learn about the stock market investment can get demotivated upon seeing a lot of technical graphs and charts shown on TV or in newspapers. But the reality is that these large financial–statistical numbers have very little to do with stock investments. The good news is that stock investment is for each one of us, irrespective of our backgrounds!

4

The Stock Market Is a Risky Ride

Myth or Reality?

In the words of William Feather, 'The funniest thing about the stock market is that every time one person buys, the other sells, and both think they are astute.'

Are you scared to lose—or have even lost—your hard-earned money in stocks? Do you treat the stock market as risky? If yes, then this chapter will be an eye-opener for you.

Too often, people think that the stock market is like gambling in a casino with a high possibility of losing all your money in seconds. But fortunately, this is not what stock market investment is. You lose money only if you are an impatient trader or lack the right approach to investing. Since you have not been taught the core logic of dealing with shares, you still find the stock market enigmatic.

Speaking from personal experience, investing is simple. Just think: If it was really rocket science, then how did people with no financial skills become multi-millionaires by merely investing in stocks? Moreover, it isn't even for the high-IQ number crunchers. Otherwise, the list of successful investors would contain only mathematicians and statisticians, which is not the case.

Here's an example to illustrate this. Can you decode this graph?

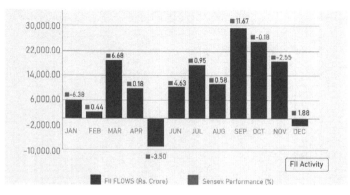

Graph showing Sensex performance over one year

The best part is that this graph doesn't need to be decoded!

A famous real-life success story of stock market investment is that of Warren Buffett, one of the richest men on Earth. He owes almost all his wealth to the profits he earned from stock investing. Ironically, without being a financial guru himself, he outperformed the best financial gurus on the planet to create his multi-billion dollar worth! It surely proves that you need not be a mathematician, a business analyst, or an accomplished statistician to make money from stocks.

Alas! The sanctity of stock investment is diluted by gamblers who gave it a casino-type image. For ages, people have believed that when they invest in stocks, their money is at stake. But fortunately, this is not so; the stock market is a sure-shot money multiplier, provided you play the game after being aware of its rules.

Unfortunately, stock market investment is still not dealt with in our education system. As students, we have never been taught 'how to invest in the stock market.' Even in business schools, stock investment is never taught, and so people are unaware of the basics of investing in stocks.

Tip: Do you treat stock investment as a monster or a friend? Whatever your strategy is, the stock market will reciprocate the same way.

How Did the Stock Market Earn a Casino Image?

Before the 1990s, the stock market in India lacked a competent regulator; there were no powerful bodies that could regulate stock market dealings. There was also a lack of a centralized or digital system to regulate stock trading. Imagine a situation where banks function without a centralized regulatory body like the Reserve Bank of India. It was as bad as that! Thus, influential stock market participants would dominate and manipulate the stock market to cater to their vested interests.

How Did the Stock Market Function in the Early Days?

Back then, stock prices were determined based on manual bidding. Due to this inefficient system, there were many unfair speculations, which helped insiders earn hefty profits. On top of that, there was no technology to verify the market news, so every report, true or false, led to stock price fluctuations.

Over a period, this tarnished the image of stock investment. In the quest to make money, the poor investors kept getting trapped and ended up losing all their hard-earned money. Such incidents gave the stock market a negative image, which prominently exists even after decades.

As they say, 'Once bitten, twice shy!' So, this explains why most people are still scared of making any investment in stocks.

Present Scenario of Stock Market Investment

On 12 April 1992, a regulatory body called the Securities and Exchange Board of India (SEBI) was formed. It would be the central controller of stocks in India, and it became a big boon for stock traders and investors. As a regulatory body, SEBI started working in the interest of all investors.

Soon after it was formed, SEBI barred unfair stock trading deals, and played a protective role in streamlining investment practices. Soon, another stock exchange called the National Stock Exchange (NSE) was formed to make the functioning of stock exchanges transparent and democratic.

With all these strict regulating bodies operating under a legal framework, stock market trading became fair and reliable once again. Though slight manipulations may still exist today, there is ample room to create huge wealth through legitimate means. Thus, it would not be wrong to say that the stock market is safe if investments are made with the right intent of investing in businesses rather than wrongly choosing to gamble for meagre profits.

It won't be wrong to say that the stock market is like a *mirror*—it reflects who you are. So be aware of your beliefs about money investment, as they will reflect on your stock trading.

5

Factors Influencing the Stock Market

How much does the stock market fluctuate? A lot! So much so that whenever you see a graph with lots of ups and downs, you think it represents the stock market.

Have you ever wondered, 'Why do stock prices fluctuate?'

A stock market is a place where you wake up to see a new trend every day. The stock prices fluctuate so frequently that the price variation is seen not every day, not every minute, but every second. But what causes it to fluctuate so much?

This volatility is caused due to the influence of various market forces, which are as follows:

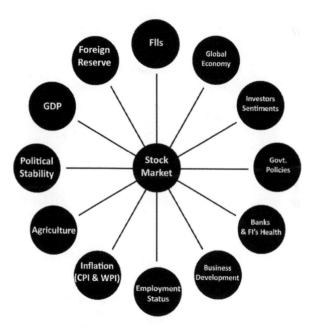

Factors affecting the stock market

- *Economic factors:* Higher economic growth or better prospects for growth will increase consumption in the economy. When people start to consume more, their spending will increase. Hence, the money flow in the market increases. This will help boost companies' earnings and, in turn, the share prices or the stock market in a broader sense. Investors will be encouraged to invest more in the stock market.

Conversely, when the economy is falling, it has a reverse effect on investors. They tend to restrict their expenses and spend only on essential items. They also withdraw money from the stock market.

- *Geopolitical factors:* Unfavourable circumstances like war, terrorism, and political unrest can negatively affect the entire business scenario. Investors and traders refrain from investing in stocks in such unfavourable situations.
- *Foreign institutional investors:* FIIs are foreign companies that invest in Indian businesses. FIIs see a great investment opportunity in growing economies like China, India, and Brazil. They prefer to invest a significant amount of wealth in the Indian stock market with the power of selling and buying anytime. Whenever FIIs withdraw their investments from the Indian market, the share market gets adversely affected.

- *Inflation:* To hedge against rising inflation, people should invest more in the stock market because no other financial instrument can give such high returns. As purchasing power decreases, buying or investing in every other commodity, be it land or a house, becomes more difficult.
- *Foreign exchange rates:* When the rates of foreign currencies fluctuate, it influences our domestic stock market. It affects the stock prices of Indian companies that have an overseas presence. Companies involved in import and export will face a major impact on their operations and share prices. For instance, when the rupee depreciates, IT and Pharma companies with an overseas presence enjoy a positive effect.
- *Demand and supply:* If an industry grows, the demand for the shares of promising companies in that industry increases. When the demand goes up, the share pricing also goes up and vice versa.
- *Investor sentiments:* The stock market is invariably governed by the feelings of the investors. If the investors are willing to take risks, then they tend to invest more and vice-versa.
- *Interest rate outlook:* When the RBI's interest rate rises, businesses' cost of borrowing increases. They are left with lower profits, causing share prices to fall since now there is less capital for further expansion and future prospects fulfilment. The distribution of dividends will also be lesser. When interest rates are reduced, the enterprises thrive, which can result in a higher share price.

However, these impacts are short term. In a country like India, interest rate fluctuations are frequent, because of which companies maintain a buffer to keep the impact on their day-to-day operations minimal.

- *Trade balance:* The trade balance reflects the difference in imports and exports of the country. If imports are more than exports, it is referred to as a trade deficit. If the imports remain higher for a prolonged period, it can push the country into debt. Hence, the trade deficit negatively impacts the economy.

  On the other hand, if the exports are more than imports, it is referred to as a trade surplus. Trade surplus reflects a healthy state of the economy and impacts the stock market positively.

These are the main factors that affect stock market investment. They also explain why the stock market keeps fluctuating all the time. However, the stock market also impacts the economy of the country.

How the Stock Market Impacts the Country's Economy

- *Effect on wealth:* If the prices of the stocks depreciate, it will discourage the buyers from investing more money in shares. If people also spend less on buying goods and products, it will bring down the country's GDP, as consumer spending is a major component of the GDP. Consequently, the stock market will go down further, negatively impacting the economy of the country. The opposite of this situation also holds true.
- *Effect on pensions:* Going by the general convention, pension funds are associated with stock market investments. If the invested funds suffer huge losses, then the pension funds of the government may struggle to keep their promises of paying regular funds to retired citizens.

6

Do Currency Fluctuations Affect the Economy of a Country?

We know that currency fluctuations directly impact the stock market of a country. But a question that always baffles naïve investors is, *'Why do currencies fluctuate at all?'* It is a most valid question that comes to the minds of all beginners who are investing in shares for the first time. As you must have seen, a few currencies rise continually to all-time highs, whereas others follow a downward spiral. So, what makes these currencies fluctuate?

A simple reason why currencies fluctuate is the variation in the supply and demand of the money. The amount of domestic currency circulating in the country's economy is majorly governed by the country's import and export values. When you are exporting or importing, the Indian currency is either flowing in or out of the state. If exports increase at a higher rate than imports, it means more revenue is earned in foreign currency. This, in turn, indicates a reduced supply of Indian currency in the international market, and consequently, we see an appreciation in the exchange rate of the rupee.

However, if the import of the country increases, it means the supply of our domestic currency increases in the exchange market, resulting in its depreciation.

An interesting question I am often asked is, 'Why does the government not print extra currency to eradicate poverty?' This is a million-dollar question that wrecks the minds of many. Good thinking! Although the rationale behind this concern is correct, the answer to this is *no*. The government cannot print extra currency at all!

Why Can't the Government Print Extra Currency?

Distributing Free Currency Will Lead to the Currency's Devaluation

The national wealth of any country is fixed, and it increases only with the growth of the economy. If the government starts distributing currency for free to the poor, then the money flow in the country increases. But the economy or the wealth of the nation remains the same. Hence, as per the demand and supply equation, the increased supply of the currency depreciates its value.

Distributing Free Currency Will Lead to Pseudo-Inflation

If there is a sudden increase in money in the system, then the demand for all goods and services will also rise subsequently. This will push their prices up further. Consequently, this leads to pseudo-inflation, which will ensure that you buy the same number of products as before but at an extra cost. Thus, in both situations, we are back to square one.

Let us understand this with the help of an example.

Suppose your monthly income is Rs 10, and you purchase one pen with it every month. Suddenly, the government tells you that it will deposit Rs 500 into your account every month. So, out of euphoria, what will you do? You have easy access to money, and thus you will naturally spend on things that you always desired. Therefore, instead of just the one pen, you bought each month, you will now buy five different pens, other stationery, some snacks, a movie ticket, etc. Your increased income will fuel your increased desires, and that will lead to increased demand for products in general.

As a thumb rule, when the demand for commodities is high, their price automatically rises, resulting in inflation. Thus, the same pen that you were earlier buying for Rs 10 will now cost you Rs 500. Hence, free currency distribution to eradicate poverty will instead create more debt.

The Story of Zimbabwe's Hyperinflation

A real example of how currency distribution creates an economic disaster was seen in Zimbabwe. The government had distributed free currency to eradicate poverty from the nation, but unfortunately, this led to hyperinflation. The prices of all commodities rose so much that with US$15, you could buy only three eggs in Zimbabwe! Let us see what exactly happened in detail.

Back in 2007, the then President of Zimbabwe, Mr Robert Mugabe, had all the right intentions to eradicate poverty from his nation. And thus, he took big pieces of land from the Whites and redistributed it equally among ethnic Zimbabweans. This led to the collapse of the banking and agricultural sectors of the country, which in turn triggered unemployment. So, the nation started printing more and more currency and distributed it widely amongst its population. But the value and faith in the currency were lost, leading to hyperinflation. The inflation rose from 19 per cent to 48 per cent in just one year! And then there was nothing left that could check this hyperinflation.

The inflation continued to rise for the next 17 years in Zimbabwe, and at one point, banknotes of denomination Z$100,000,000 were needed for simple daily needs! This was a big lesson for all the countries worldwide that may have thought of eradicating poverty by printing more currency.

Finally, Zimbabwe had to switch to a foreign currency to bring prices back to normal. But it took the Zimbabweans a long time to overcome the financial crisis.

Is Currency Devaluation Always Harmful?

The most logical answer to this question is *yes,* but this is not always true in reality! Currency devaluation may not always turn out to be harmful to the country. In fact, the effect of currency devaluation is always valued against the balance of trade of the country. If the country's exports are higher than its imports, then the foreign reserves of the nation increase. Hence, the currency value appreciates and vice-versa.

So, when a nation's currency depreciates, it sets an alert to push exports, which otherwise get ignored. Therefore, it is wrong to say that currency devaluation is harmful all the time. If the currency devaluation is handled well, it, in turn, pushes the exports, increasing foreign reserves.

7

Stock Investment versus Other Financial Investments

I'm sure you will agree that gold is always the first choice whenever we wish to invest our excess money. If the excess is huge, then definitely the choice to invest is in land. There are other options available as well. But are we really aware which of these assets will fetch the maximum returns?

The information below will be quite useful to you if you belong to the majority of people who are unaware of the exact return on assets.

How Do Debentures, Property, Gold, and Equity Investments Work?

Debentures

While investing in debentures, you get a fixed rate of interest, but you don't get a share of the profits earned by the company. Here, your returns are limited to just 'fixed returns'; plus, you get back the principal sum invested.

Property

Investing in property demands a massive amount of capital. There are many parameters for a property to be liquid, such as location, the type of land, etc. It takes a lot of time for the property to appreciate its value. Therefore, for you to fetch substantial returns, you will have to be patient and stay invested for a long duration.

Gold

Gold serves as the primary attraction for all investors looking to gain a substantial amount of money. Over the past several decades, the increase in demand for gold has led to a considerable appreciation in its value. But sadly, there is not much use for the gold, as the money gets trapped unless the possessed gold is liquidated. Moreover, no business basics can be applied to gold to grow the money further.

Equity

Equity is perceived as a riskier investment bet than various other asset classes such as gold, land, and bonds. But in reality, it is a much better option due to its accessibility, liquidity, historically better returns, etc.

Equity investment is by far the best investment option, as by buying stakes in a company, you become an owner of the company. Just as business owners earn profits in businesses, similarly in equity investment, you are the first-hand receiver of the company's profits. Moreover, returns on equity fetch you a much better profit percentage as compared to other asset classes, as you also bear the risk of loss by being a part-owner of the business.

Thus, equity investment does outperform other popular asset investments such as gold or land, provided you invest your money with the right approach. Now, let us see how much return each of these asset classes gave in the last 18 years.

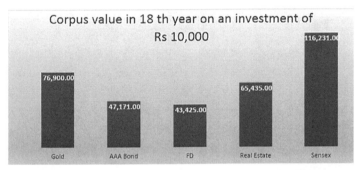

CAGR return on different asset classes in the last 18 years from 2001 to 2019

Showing the rate of return on the corpus amount over a time period of 18 years

	Gold	AAA Bond	FD	Real Estate	Sensex
Corpus Amount	Rs 76,900	Rs 47,171	Rs 43,425	Rs 65,435	Rs 116,231
Rate of return (in per cent)	12	9	8.5	11	14.6

From the graph on p. 36, it is evident that gold fetched almost 12 per cent returns, the real estate brought 11 per cent returns, FD fetched 8.5 per cent returns, AAA bonds (debentures) fetched 9 per cent returns, but Sensex topped the list with more than 14 per cent returns. So, stock investment can get you the highest returns. You won't get this sort of return with any other investment class such as gold, property, or debt.

The worst thing is that investing in stocks is still considered to be the last option in India.

Other Benefits of Stock Investment besides Promising Returns

- Long-term capital gains are taxed at a lower rate.
- Stock investment brings in regular income as dividends, and the value of the invested capital also appreciates with time. Moreover, returns in stocks have historically been far higher than in other asset classes.
- Gold can be stolen, and property can be occupied illegally. But there are no such threats in stock investment.
- The stock market offers high liquidity and ease of transaction.

So, do equities outperform other asset classes every time?
The straightforward answer is '*no*.' Though equities have impressively outperformed other asset classes in the past, they still cannot beat *all the asset classes, all the time.*

Compounding: The Force behind Wealth Creation in Stocks

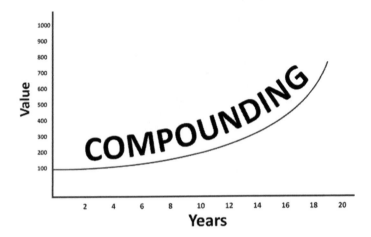

Do you know that with the power of compounding, the small investments you make today go on to bear huge profits over time?

What Is Compounding?

Compounding is a process in which an investment's earnings—that are earned either from capital appreciation or from interest—are reinvested to generate additional income over time. This growth is calculated using exponential functions and occurs because earnings would be generated from both the initial principal amount and the accumulated earnings.

In school, we used this equation:

$A = P (1+R/100)^N$
Where A = Amount, P = Principal, R = Rate of return, N = Number of years

The same equation can now be presented as

$$F = I (1+CAGR/100)^T$$
Where F = Final amount, I = Initial amount, CAGR = Compounded Annual Growth Rate, T= Time (number of years)

In simple words, compounding is similar to compound interest and is referred to as compounded annual growth rate. In compounding, you earn profits in two ways:

1. From the principal value
2. From the additional earnings through interest which are reinvested to give magnified returns.

No wonder compounding is called the 'interest of interest.' *It has the magical power to magnify a small investment in the long run, which is why it is referred to as the 8th wonder of the world.*

How Does Compounding Work?

We are all caught in a rat race of multiplying our money every day. To meet our financial goals, we tend to save more and spend less. While saving is essential, its rewards can be compounded if we invest our savings intelligently. So, let's understand how this works.

For example, let's suppose you have Rs 10,000, and you invest it in a fixed deposit at a rate of 7 per cent interest per annum.

An example of how compounding affects your money

Particulars	Withdrawing your interest component	Reinvesting your interest component
Investment value	Rs 10,000	Rs 10,000
Interest rate P.A.	7%	7%
Time period	30 years	30 years
Total interest income	Rs 21,000	Rs 66,000
Total wealth	Rs 31,000	Rs 76,000
Money is multiplied by	3.1 times	7.6 times

Due to the compounding effect, the initial amount of Rs 10,000 has become Rs 76,000 in 30 years just by keeping it in fixed deposits. Now, if you had invested the same sum of money in a simple interest-bearing instrument, or if you had withdrawn your interest on an annual basis, your corpus would have been Rs 31,000 in 30 years, which is less than half of the former. The difference is clearly visible from the graph shown next.

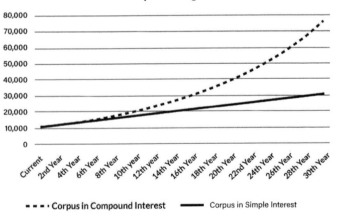

Compounding effect over 30 years

From this example, it is clear that compounded returns significantly outperform the returns gained from simple interest. Hence, to meet your long-term goals, it is imperative to invest your money in financial assets like stocks to get compounded returns.

Let us understand this with an example. Suppose you have to save for your child's higher education.

Growth of your investment in FD over 20 years

Particulars	Amount
Cost of education as per today's value	Rs 8 lakh
Your saving (kept in an FD)	Rs 8 lakh
Time period (need this for child's higher education)	20 years
Rate of return on FD	7%
Inflation rate	6%
Tax rate	30%
Maturity value of your investment after 20 years	Rs 30.95 lakh
Post-tax corpus value	Rs 21.67 lakh
Cost of education after 20 years (after inflation)	Rs 25.65 lakh
Deficit	Rs 3.98 lakh

As you can see from the table, you had the required corpus for your child's education as per today's cost (Rs 8 lakh). But you need the money after 20 years when your child is actually ready for higher education. So you invested the money in a fixed deposit for 20 years. Now, take a look at the returns after considering inflation and taxation. After making the calculation, you found that your investment has ended up with a deficit of Rs 3.98 lakh.

So, do you see how ineffective it is to invest money in a fixed deposit? When you have long-term goals like your child's education or marriage, buying a house or a car, retirement, etc., keeping your money in a savings account or fixed deposit will definitely not work.

How Much Can You Earn?

Let's see how much your corpus would have been if you had put your money in an index fund.

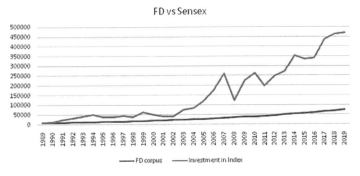

Comparison between investing in FDs and index funds

From the graph, it is clear that the Sensex was at a level of 778 in 1989, and now, it is trading at a level of 36,600. This is nearly 14 per cent CAGR for 30 years, which is double of your FD returns. So, your investment worth Rs 10,000 would have been around Rs 4.7 crore if you had just replicated the index, i.e., 617 times of your fixed deposit corpus.

The market generally offers an average return of 14–15 per cent per annum. But if you select stocks carefully, you can even surpass the market return.

Let's understand this with examples.

Example 1: Wipro

If a person had invested Rs 10,000 in 1980, the money would have become approximately Rs 550 crore in 2018.

How is it possible?

In 1980, the face value of a Wipro share was Rs 100. Let's assume you have bought 100 shares at that price. So, the total investment would have been Rs 10,000.

Growth of number of Wipro shares from 1980 to 2018

Year	Action	No. of shares
1980	Initial investment	100
1981	Bonus 1:1	200
1985	Bonus 1:1	400
1986	Stock split to FV from Rs 100 to Rs 10	4,000
1987	Bonus 1:1	8,000
1989	Bonus 1:1	16,000
1992	Bonus 1:1	32,000
1995	Bonus 1:1	64,000
1997	Bonus 2:1	1,92,000
1999	Stock split to FV from Rs 10 to Rs 2	9,60,000
2004	Bonus 2:1	28,80,000
2005	Bonus 1:1	57,60,000
2010	Bonus 2:3	96,00,000

So, your investment worth Rs 10,000 has become Rs 550 crore in 38 years, i.e., with a CAGR of 42 per cent.

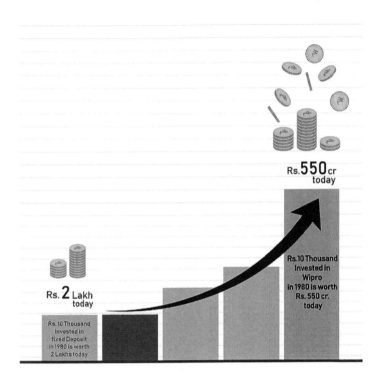

Example 2: Eicher Motors

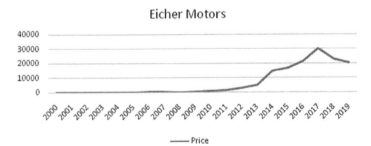

Growth of Eicher Motors share price over 20 years

As you can see from the graph in Example 2, an investment of Rs 50,000 in Eicher Motors shares in 1998 would have become Rs 10.5 crore by 2019. The company was trading for Rs 10.70 in 1998, and the current market price is around Rs 21,000, generating a CAGR return of nearly 46.5 per cent in 20 years.

These examples emphasize the importance of compounding and how staying invested in stocks helps earn excellent returns in the long term. Also, these examples show the importance of investing in stocks that outweighs the returns from FDs or the interest earned from a savings account.

Long-term investment returns of selected companies

Stock	Period of investment		Amount Invested (Rs)	Final amount	No. of years	Price	
	From	To				Multiple	CAGR (%)
Infosys	June 1993	October 2017	10,000	2,97,30,645	24.0	2,973	39
Emami	October 1995	October 2017	10,000	52,28,958	22.0	523	33
Eicher Motors	January 1990	October 2017	10,000	2,01,79,688	27.5	2,018	32
Shree Cement	January 1990	October 2017	10,000	1,91,27,722	27.5	1,913	32
Sun Pharma	December 1994	October 2017	10,000	26,10,377	23.0	261	27
HDFC Bank	May 1995	October 2017	10,000	22,46,957	22.5	225	27
HDFC	January 1990	October 2017	10,000	48,78,143	28.0	488	25

Stock	Period of investment		Amount Invested (Rs)	Final amount	No. of years	Price	
	From	To				Multiple	CAGR (%)
Asian Paints	January 1988	October 2017	10,000	59,03,500	30.0	590	24
Britannia Industries	January 1988	October 2017	10,000	56,83,802	30.0	568	24

Source: Economic Times

Warren Buffett: A Live Example of Achieving Mega Success from Stock Investment

What did Warren Buffett do to become a billionaire from the stock investment?

Warren Buffett, also called 'The Oracle of Omaha,' is no genius. He merely discovered the power of compounding, which led him to build an asset worth 87 billion dollars.

The wisest thing that Warren Buffett did, which led to his becoming a multi-billionaire, was that he invested in shares at a very early age, which compounded annually at 20 per cent for 70 long years.

Here's how he could create such significant wealth.

1. Buffett started investing at the young age of 11 years and bought six shares of an oil company at $38 each. Though he eventually sold those shares at $40 each, he soon saw that the prices of each of those shares rebounded to $200. It got Warren thinking about the value of timing in trading shares. It is this value of timing that made him what he is today.

2. Soon after doing some research, Buffett invested in the shares of Berkshire Hathaway in 1962. And guess what? He held those shares for many decades and is still going

strong! Currently, those very shares are worth millions of dollars with the magic of compounding.

Our learning: Warren Buffett is no genius (only in this context), but he understood the value of investing in good stocks for a long term, and that made him super-rich today.

Consistency Is More Important Than Outperformance

The consistency of returns is an important factor in letting compounding work efficiently. If the returns on a stock are not consistent each year, then the results from compounding are not as effective. Let us understand this with the following example:

Suppose there are two stocks, Stock A and Stock B. Stock A gives lesser returns but is consistent in approach, whereas Stock B gives higher returns but is inconsistent.

Comparison of returns of Stock A and Stock B

	Stock A		Stock B	
	Market price	Year on year return	Market price	Year on year return
Purchase date	100	–	250	–
1st year	120	20%	350	40%
2nd year	138	15%	300	-14%
3rd year	168	22%	220	-27%
4th year	195	16%	300	36%
5th year	222	14%	350	17%
	Total returns in 5 years	87%	**Total returns in 5 years**	52%

You can see that Stock A has outperformed Stock B due to its consistency in returns. It shows that the power of compounding works efficiently when the returns are consistent.

The stock market is a place where consistent investments for an extended period definitely pay off. But staying invested for an extended period comes with its challenges, such as the following:

- You must stay invested even when the stock market has crashed.
- You must refrain from selling stocks when the stocks are trading at excellent prices. History has proven that staying invested consistently over a long period is essential instead of disinvesting to encash the extra profits when the stock outperforms.

Wealth Creation in Stocks through the Power of Compounding

Compounding works best when you buy good stocks that are undervalued and stay invested in them for an extended period. If you understand this critical benefit of long-term investment, then you will never be tempted towards gambling.

The following graph shows the business life cycle indicating the various phases that occur in every business.

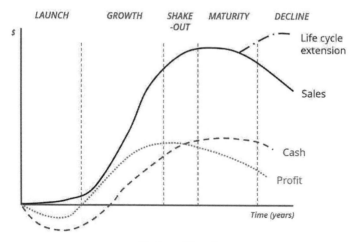

Business life cycle

Every business follows a life cycle comprising the launch phase, the growth phase, the shake-out phase, the maturity phase, and the decline phase. *As an investor, your job is to find a fast-growing company that is in the growth phase but whose stock is valued like a slow-growing company. This means you should buy shares of a promising company whose shares are trading at a price lower than their fair price.*

The underlying principle of stock investment states that your profits are defined by the price at which you procure a stock. The company you choose can be the best in the world, but you will make good profits only if you buy its stocks at the right price. For example, companies such as Britannia, HUL, and Asian Paints, appear to be likely bets, but their shares are highly overpriced. Thus, the stock value of these companies might not serve as a profitable investment option.

Hence, I would like to repeat, 'You must look for a company which is in the growth phase, but its shares must be trading at a lower price similar to the shares of a company in its launch phase.' Or, you must look for a company in the maturity phase offering shares at a value equivalent to the company in the growth phase, and so on.

The Rule of 72

The rule of 72 is widely applied by all financial analysts and stock investment firms to calculate their income on the investments made. It states that for an investment to double, the formula is as follows:

Double returns = 72/rate of return

For example, if the rate of interest is 10 per cent, then in how many years will your money double?

Double returns = 72/10 = 7.2 years

Hence, your money will double in 7.2 years.
Or if the rate of interest is 18 per cent, then,

Double returns = 72/18 = 4 years

Hence, your money will double in four years.
The major drawback of using this rule is that it is restricted to calculating only double returns on the investment value. If you are looking at exhaustive returns, then the power of compounding is always available as an option.

1. Compounding works in the long run, only when the investor stays invested even when the stock prices have taken an unexpected dip.
2. The stock market has multiple winners and losers at any point in time as it gives a chance to win or lose concurrently.

8

The Psychology behind Stock Investment

Stock market investment is for anyone who has the willingness and patience to learn the art of investing. People from all backgrounds and professions like computer professionals, teachers, architects, designers, astronauts, homemakers, students, artists, restaurateurs, etc., can learn how to invest in stocks.

Learning how to invest in stocks will make you far wiser in your investment deals. As I always keep saying, stocks are sure-shot money multipliers, provided you know how to play the game. But there is a lot more to stock investment than just trading, which you will understand once you read further. You will be surprised at how exciting it is to learn how to observe, analyse, and react to the stock market.

The Psychology of a Naïve Investor

The following is a list of common beliefs from the world of investing. See if you have them too!

- You look at stock market investment as a money-making tool rather than as a means to create wealth.
- You have low risk-taking ability. You prefer to invest in low-priced stocks, assuming that the risks involved are also lower, without knowing the credentials of the companies.
- You operate with a fear psychology and refrain from investing in high-priced stocks even if those stocks are promising, due to your fear of sustaining losses.
- You believe in selling off shares too early because of your fear of losing money in case the market fluctuates.

If you hold any of these beliefs, there is nothing to worry about, as these beliefs come naturally when you start as a stock investor. But you're lucky to have picked up this book, as you will see how experienced and renowned investors approach stock investment.

The Psychology of a Smart Investor

The smart investor has already burnt his fingers by losing in the quest to earn more. It is this experience of losing money that turns a naïve investor into a seasoned one. As the wise men say, there are always two ways of learning:

- The first is by making mistakes and learning from them.
- The second is by learning from the mistakes made by others.

Intelligent people, however, always tend to learn from the mistakes made by others. So, you must imitate the wiser of the lot and learn from their experiences.

Here Is What You Need to Learn

The points below are crucial to remember as you start your journey as an investor. You can think of them as thumb rules.

- Before investing in any stock, you need to conduct a detailed fundamental analysis of the company. It is the best and the most reliable way of investing.
- Your next-door neighbours or your well-meaning relatives can never be your investment advisors. Although they might be most convincing and influencing, they cannot always be your best financial advisors. And, while you may not think so at present, after you have finished reading this book, you will agree that you are your own best financial decision-maker.
- When you invest in stocks of companies, you must attentively read all the news related to those companies. But just in case you come across a piece of information that appears to be insider information, then be sure that it is deliberately made public. A retail investor can be assured of the fact that if insider information has reached him, it is because it was intended to do so.
- The electronic media, financial dailies, and online portals are not information-driven, but are instead hired to keep making noise. Another way of putting this is that the media disguises noise as information. The intent is only to keep you hooked. By the way, have you ever wondered that since these news channels have been around for 20 years, they must have made you a master of stock investment by now? But have you come anywhere close to learning the basics of stock investment?

Unlike in science, there is no fixed formula in stock investment to make profits, nor can you control the key factors to get your desired outcome. Stock market gains cannot be calculated in advance using any fixed formula or equation. Stock market investment is an art that needs to be learnt with experience and knowledge.

9

Understanding Stock Investment
Strategically

Investing in stocks comes with its own set of rules and conventions. If you have to perform too many calculations before buying a stock, then it's usually not worth investing in that stock. Usually, it is human psychology that if you spend long hours researching a product, then you somehow become convinced about buying it.

There are various aspects to stock investment. Every company will have its specific challenges related to the sector it belongs to. As an investor, you must understand the industry-specific challenges, as the challenges to survive in business differ from industry to industry.

For example, the CEO of Apple needs to continually forecast, innovate and break his head over research and development, as the products will sustain in the market only if the relevant innovation is brought in. But the CEO of Coca-Cola has to maintain the same old product and increase its market share across the globe. The challenge there lies in not changing the product at all and still ensuring its relevance in changing times. Each business comes with its own set of broad challenges, and you must understand the basics of that business before investing in it.

As successful leading investors put it, *'The safest bet is to invest in a business that even an idiot can run, because someday an idiot will run it.'*

For example, if you have two options, Coca-Cola and Apple, investing in Coca-Cola will be safer than investing in Apple. Remember, I am using the word 'safer', not 'more rewarding'. Which stock is right for you depends on your objectives.

Qualities You DON'T Need to Be a Good Investor

- High IQ
- Technical, mathematical, and accounting skills
- Expensive software to analyse complex graphs and charts

Qualities You DO Need to Be a Good Investor

- Patience
- Courage to go against the market trends
- Learning ability
- Emotional stability
- Willingness to give up short-term desires to build enormous wealth in the future

These qualities are needed due to the nature of the stock market, which is highly fluctuating and unpredictable.

10

Value Investing

The Investment Strategy to Get Better Return on Investment

The concept of 'value investing' was developed by Benjamin Graham and David Dodd in 1934. Value investing is a tested philosophy used by stock investment experts like Charlie Munger, Warren Buffett, and Peter Lynch.

These investors have been able to create immense wealth from stock investment only by using value investing. This concept is simple and sustainable and can be followed across the globe.

> *'In the short run, the market is a voting machine, but in the long run, it is a weighing machine.'*
>
> —Benjamin Graham

The aim of value investing is to buy stocks that are under-priced due to market dynamics. Value investors constantly search for stocks that are sold at a value less than their fair value.

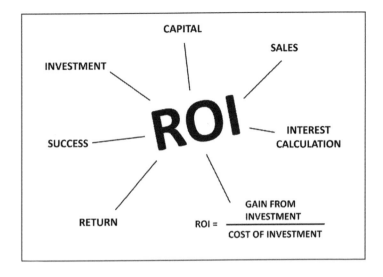

What's the Big Deal about Value Investing?

1. Value investing has a proven track record of more than 60 years. All the big names such as Benjamin Graham, Warren Buffett, Charlie Munger, and Peter Lynch, have created wealth through it.
2. It is a tried and tested formula across global markets and in all market conditions.
3. Value investing has helped investors earn index-beating returns consistently.
4. The concept of value investing is based on extremely logical and sensible assumptions.
5. It is simple to understand and can be practised by both full-time and part-time investors, as well as beginners without much accounting knowledge.

Value Investing Is Based on the Following Assumptions

Going by the thumb rule, the best way to judge any theory is to examine its assumptions. Value investing, like most other approaches, has a set of assumptions. Let's analyse them.

1. Every stock has an intrinsic value attached to it. This intrinsic value is the actual value of the company, calculated by considering all tangible and intangible aspects of the company.
2. Every stock eventually trades around its fair value in the long run.
3. Markets are not entirely efficient in the short run.

The father of value investing, Benjamin Graham, who was also Warren Buffett's teacher, explained that in the long run, the market rewards the good companies and punishes the bad companies. Therefore, it is always suggested not to look at the frequent price fluctuations in stocks while investing.

Often, it is seen that investors start with good, positive intentions, but when they see their friends earning more with risky trades, they dump their investing philosophy and start copying others' behaviour. Such things might be rewarding in the short run, but they will prove deadly in the long term!

Was Your Stock Purchase a Good Deal?

The price you pay for the stock is what makes it a good buy or a bad one. For example, if you buy an iPhone at a 40 per cent discount, that is a great purchase, but when you buy the same

iPhone for anything higher than its labelled price, it becomes a bad purchase.

Fortunately, in the physical world, we have the concept of maximum retail price or sticker price, wherein the product's price is decided by the company that owns it. *But in the stock market, the price is determined by people like you and me, and therefore, there is no fixed price that is fair. It is up to the individual to conduct their calculations and decide the fair price of the stock they want to buy.*

So, for investor X, the fair price of Maruti Suzuki could be Rs 1,000, while for investor Y, it could be Rs 500. This shows that what's expensive for me might not be expensive for you or somebody else.

Choosing the price of a stock is similar to how players are auctioned in IPL or EPL. Every team bids for the players according to its expectations from them. The higher the expectations, the higher the price they are willing to pay. Similarly, if you expect fantastic performance from a company in the coming years, you would be willing to pay a far higher price. Since everyone's expectations are different, the estimates of a fair price are also different.

Every stock has a fair value that shows a range within which you think it is a reasonable buy. And I am sure you will agree that we don't buy anything without checking its price. So why should it be different for stocks? In later chapters, we will study how to calculate the fair price of a stock, based on your expectations from the company.

Benjamin Graham's Beliefs on Value Investing

Benjamin Graham believed that any investment without a surety of good returns is called speculating and not investing. As per his definition of investing, investing necessarily comprises the following two traits:

1. The investment must be safe at all times, and
2. The returns on the investment must be adequate

Let us discuss these two traits in detail.

The Investment Must Be Safe at All Times

What we investors understand as 'risk' is often just uncertainty or volatility. We assess risk based on market fluctuations or volatility rather than gauging the actual risk. But when it comes to serious investing, the risk is only when you are not able to achieve your desired returns. It has got nothing to do with current stock price fluctuations.

Now, let us understand this with the following two graphs depicting the variations in the stock price over a period of time.

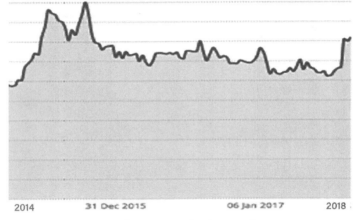

| 2014 | 31 Dec 2015 | 06 Jan 2017 | 2018 |

Movement of a certain stock price over three years

From this graph, it is evident that the share price has not fluctuated much, which means the share price is not volatile. But another point to note from the graph is that the stock price has not increased in the last three years. So would you not consider this a risk? Yes, of course! Because your ultimate motto of earning from this investment is not served.

Now let's look at the next graph.

Here the stock price has been fluctuating, indicating huge volatility, but the share price has increased from Rs 900 to Rs 1,600. Here, although there is high fluctuation in the pricing, in the end, the investors' profits are ensured.

Movement of another stock price over three years

So, by looking at these two graphs, we can conclude that risk and volatility are two different things and should not be confused with each other.

Investment Tip: Never buy stocks by merely looking at the prices. Get into the core analysis of a company to understand its true worth before investing a single penny in it.

The Return on Investment Must Be Adequate

Investing, when done for a long period, is considered to be safe. The only concern in long-term investing is whether it brings you adequate returns or not.

The word 'adequate' can never be justified, as the expectation of each investor varies. For example, a mere

7 per cent return on an FD can be a good investment for me, but the same does not hold true for somebody expecting a 20 per cent return on the same value.

Hence, for any monetary investment to qualify as an 'investment,' it must be free from the risk of losing money (read, minimal risk of losing money), and it must fetch satisfactory returns for the investor.

11

Stock Investment Strategy

The big names like Warren Buffett and Charlie Munger have mesmerized the entire world by creating immense fortunes through stock investment. Of course, each of us wants to know the critical facets of stock investment that can help us mint money like them. Here are a few aspects that will give you some insights.

- Stock investment is an art that needs to be learnt, and its principles are pretty simple and worth remembering. Stock investment can fetch you huge wealth, provided you learn to invest.
- Though trading is very risky, you will still see the majority of people entering the stock markets only to trade.
- There is no surety of returns in trading. At times you will see speculators making a lot of money in stocks, and at other times you will find them losing all of it.
- Sometimes even after thorough research and analysis, you will not be able to make the expected money, and you

may even incur losses. This is normal, which is why I say, 'Stock investment is an art.'

The above-mentioned points are related to investing. But since you will invest in the stock market, here are a few aspects related to the market.

- The stock market is a transparent trading medium providing equal opportunities to all investors and businesses.
- The stock market is highly irrational, and stock prices can fluctuate suddenly from high to low, and vice-versa, without any prior indication.
- There is no need to hurry to pick stocks as the stock market brings a new deal each day. When a bull market begins, the bear market ends and vice-versa, and this cycle keeps repeating. So, you get ample opportunities regularly to invest or disinvest in stocks.
- In the stock market, trading depends on breaking news of the market, resulting in a fall and rise in stock prices every day. But if you approach stock investment as a wealth creator, then such market distractions will be of little help.
- You must have seen or heard of many stock investment disasters. Such events happen due to the following reasons:

  a. Investors anticipate huge returns and spend way too much money at once, increasing the risk of losing it all.
  b. Investors choose stocks on shared tips and popularity, not based on the true valuation of the stocks.

c. Investors tend to buy and sell stocks with corresponding market fluctuations, which are often non-productive.

d. Over diversification of portfolio might not fetch productive returns.

- The stock market has just two extreme perspectives: favourable and unfavourable. Typically, in *favourable circumstances*, you see a 'high buy-sell price,' and in *unfavourable circumstances*, you see a 'low buy-sell price.'

- I believe the intelligent approach is always:

  - When speculators/traders buy, you must *hold*.
  - When speculators/traders sell, you must *buy*.

I know this may not make much sense to you at this point of time, but this is explained in detail in further chapters.

- Always remember that there are two aspects to money-making, which are:

1. Risks
2. Rewards

The rewards should always be higher than the perceived risks. If the perceived risk is higher than the expected returns in the current market scenario, then the investor must evaluate the market and refrain from picking new stocks. This is because any wrong investments may result in losing all the money earned so far.

- For each investor, every new transaction either teaches a new lesson or increases conviction in the old one.
- Another good thing about the stock market is that you can afford to make a few mistakes as long as you make the right investments the rest of the time. Your good investments will overshadow the few errors you make.
- If an investor has been lucky enough to fetch good returns for a few initial years or more consecutively, then they usually think of themselves as confident investors. This overconfidence often gives unfavourable results, as the investors take high, uncalculated risks to earn more.
- Stock investment is indeed one of the most promising and most rewarding businesses ever. It gives you the huge benefit of making money without getting involved in the business. There is no headache of running the business and taking care of its various aspects, yet you get great profit from it. You leave your hard-earned money in some of the safest hands of visionaries like Azim Premji, and Ratan Tata. And all that business ever needs is the right people to drive it with the right approach to make it successful. So your money surely is in the safest hands!
- Stock investment is a flexible way of making money, as you have the liberty of buying multiple stocks of all promising companies from different sectors.
- While in a full-fledged business, you need anything from a few months to a few years to shut down, you can exit from your equity investment in only a few seconds, with just one click. Isn't this a great deal to place your bets on?
- The profits earned from stock investment are non-linear. In stock market investment, the expenses are linear as they have to be paid every month, but the profits come

in irregularly depending on how your invested stocks are doing. So the benefits accumulate for years together to fetch you a substantial income over time.

Staying invested in the stock market for a long time is the basic success mantra. Warren Buffett would have never become 'The Warren Buffett' if he had sold Coca-Cola in two months or even two years. He became the richest man on Earth because:

- He Bought Good Stocks and bought them at reasonable prices.
- He held those stocks for 10 years or more.

Investment Tips:

1. Did you know that out of the total investments made, only 10 per cent genuinely contributes towards wealth creation and the rest 90 per cent goes to waste? This happens with all investors, including the big names in the business.
2. Successful stock market investors are continuous learners. There are *no experts* in stock market investment.

So, What Is the Success Mantra?

Money-making in the stock market is essential but being able to retain the earned money is even more critical. An investor needs to hold on to a stock if it has doubled in its value because the power of compounding will multiply its worth many times over the years. Instead of selling the stock, the investor must look at buying more shares of the same company if he sees excellent business prospects ahead.

Warren Buffett suggests a simple strategy. Imagine you were given just 20 travel tickets to travel for a lifetime. And every time you travel, you would exhaust one travel card. So, what would your approach to travelling be? Would you not think a hundred times before travelling, as you have *only* 20 chances to travel?

Of course! This is exactly how an experienced investor thinks! He performs an in-depth analysis only to pick assured stocks. It is the level of maturity and understanding that segregates an experienced investor from a beginner. All successful investors invest in a company as the company's owner and not just as mere investors.

12

The Two Approaches to Investing

Value investing is more of an art and less of a science. Although there are no rigid rules for investing, there is a basic framework that needs to be followed.

For example, let's consider a sport like cricket. It has a few basic rules, but players are free to play the way they want. Both Rahul Dravid and Virender Sehwag were highly successful batsmen despite their contrasting playing styles. Similarly, if you know the basic rules in investing, you are free to experiment and develop your own style.

The Two Approaches

The question that knocks on the minds of most investors is, 'which stock to invest in?' Out of the 5,000-plus listed companies, how can you choose the best stocks? You cannot analyse all the listed companies; that's impossible. So how would you select the companies you do want to analyse? Here are the two ways to do it:

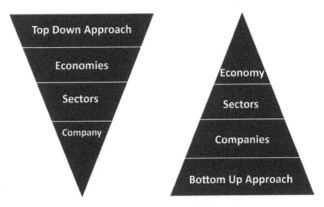

The two approaches to investing

Top-Down Approach

In the top-down approach, you first select a particular sector to invest in, and then the best company in that sector.

To select the sector, the following parameters are used:

- *Is the sector out of favour?* Check if your chosen sector has faced problems in the past. You must carefully invest in the company if you see good growth of the sector in the future despite all odds.
- *Future growth:* Check the future growth of the sector. For example, driverless cars and e-commerce will surely grow in the future.
- *Change in government regulations:* The government can come up with new regulatory laws to favour a particular sector. For example, the government imposed anti-dumping duty on tyres, which helped protect Indian tyre companies from cheap Chinese products.

- *Technology improvements:* Sometimes, a new technological intervention can benefit the entire sector. For example, increased use of solar panels made solar power companies more powerful.

Bottom-Up Approach

This is the exact opposite of the top-down approach. Here, you don't look for a particular sector; rather, you are open to buying stocks from any industry. In the bottom-up approach, you choose those stocks that meet your valuation criteria. In this approach, you can select stocks through the following:

- *Known companies:* Look for companies whose products you like, such as Colgate, Bata, and Gillette. Choosing companies based on products makes sense because, as a consumer, you know if the products sold by these companies are liked by people or not.
- *Companies related to your job:* If you are a doctor, pharma companies are a good bet. If you are a software engineer, IT companies are a good bet. Opting for these companies makes sense, as you will have a lot of knowledge about companies related to your profession.
- *News:* Newspapers, magazines, and even advertisements function as a tool to bring new companies to your notice. If you find that a new car has suddenly gotten a lot of media attention, or you see too many of them on the roads, it's usually a nice idea to start researching about the company.

Which of the Two Approaches Is Correct?

The best part of investing is that you have the freedom to decide how to invest as per your preferences. Please remember, irrespective of the approach you choose, the process of analysing the stock remains unchanged. (This will be elaborated in the next chapter.) These approaches will just help you shortlist the stocks to help the research process become easier.

13

How to Analyse Stocks in Order to Find the Good Ones

Life, as we know, is highly unpredictable. But if you stay disciplined and focused, you can achieve the significant components of your life like success, health, and family goals. Likewise, if you approach investing with a focused approach, you can create enormous wealth. Fortunately, there are always a few things you can do to increase your probability of success in investment.

Now, let us break down the process of analysing a stock in detail. This chapter and the following chapters describe a detailed holistic process of analysing stocks. Let's start with the essential components of stock analysis.

Value investing in stocks breaks down to the components given in the following figure.

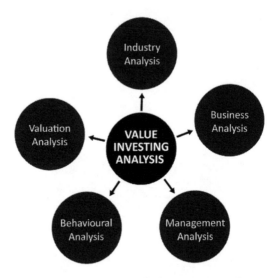

The various components of value investing analysis

Let us discuss each of the analytical components, namely industrial analysis, business analysis, management, valuation, and behavioural analysis, separately in detail.

Industry Analysis

A fish is always limited by the size of its pond. So, as an investor, you don't want to enter into an industry that is not growing. You are here to make money but to do so, it is imperative to get the process right. You need to understand the industry, how it is performing, what its positives and negatives are. All this will sum up to give you a fair idea of how much the industry will prosper in the future, which will ultimately decide your investment's profits.

Interestingly, each industry has a set of parameters to gauge its performance. For instance, a company's book value is highly important in banking or real estate stocks, while it is not required in the IT sector. For telecom companies, the Average Revenue Per User (ARPU) is taken into account, while for the commodity sector, the production cost or book value is considered.

So, how can you figure out the parameters required to gauge an industry? To help you with this, there is a theory called Porter's Five Forces model, which has been explained in a separate chapter later.

Business Analysis

As an investor, you need to develop a keen eye to analyse businesses whose shares you pick up. Every business comes with its own set of pluses and minuses. And one business can be entirely different from another even within the same sector. For example, Tech Mahindra focuses on telecom software, while Accelaya makes software solutions for airline industries. Now, whether you should buy Mahindra or Accelaya depends on whether you are optimistic about the airline or telecom industry. So, while both these companies fall under the IT sector, the reality is very different, because one IT company can contrast the other. Thus, business analysis helps us understand and interpret the business model of a company. This has been discussed in detail in a separate chapter.

Management Analysis

> 'When a manager with a reputation for brilliance tackles a business with a reputation for bad economics, the reputation of the business remains intact.'
>
> —Warren Buffett

The top management is the key driver of a business. The growth of a company depends on the capability of the top management. Thus, to identify good stocks, you need to evaluate all the intangible and tangible factors of the company, and one of the intangible factors is the company's management.

Why should you evaluate the management of the company?

The top management includes the high-level executives of the firm, such as directors, chief executive officer (CEO), and chief financial officer (CFO). When we talk about a company having good or bad control, we refer to its top officials who have the decision-making power. As shareholders, you are the owners of the company that is run and managed by the top management. Hence it is crucial to evaluate them before investing in the company.

Honestly, it is not very easy to assess the top management of a company, as most of its aspects are intangible. Moreover, the performance of senior management has to be measured in both good times and bad, which is highly time-consuming. But history has proved that smart investors have made the right judgements, which led them to invest wisely. Their immense worth generated from stock investments undoubtedly goes on to say that where there is a will, there is a way!

The key parameters to evaluate the management of a company have been discussed in detail in a separate chapter of this book.

Behavioural Analysis

As individuals, we make rational decisions, but even when we act in our best interests, many of our judgements prove to be wrong. This is because we take decisions from an emotional space deep inside us.

While charting the course of life, we gain many experiences—both good and bad—and learnings along the way, these experiences define our likes and dislikes, feelings, and emotions that sum up to form our opinions and interpretations. So, behavioural biases, consisting of opinions, feelings, perceptions, and emotions, get in our way of making rational decisions. They also show up clearly when we choose stocks.

The biggest drawback of having these biases is that they overshadow the facts and misguide our investments. Hence, to overcome these biases, one must know how various biases work and how they influence our decisions in daily life.

Have you ever noticed that any loss pricks you harder than your gains? If you think about it, you'll find that you remember the loss for a longer period than the gains. In stock investment, too, *the loss of an investor pricks him twice as hard as the joy of gains.*

In the financial world, this belief is presented in the form of a theory called Prospect Theory, which states that *our perceived loss is different from our perceived gain. The fact remains that loss and gain arouse different intensities of sadness and comfort in an investor.* Of course, this feeling of pleasure and pain influences your next investment move.

Valuation Analysis

Valuation analysis is done to estimate the approximate worth of a business. It uses a scientific approach to analyse the assets of a business, though there is a bit of art involved in it as well. By using this tool, you can find out the growth margins, capital expenses, profits, financing choices, etc.

Valuation analysis helps in figuring out the intrinsic value of a share. It is a great tool to compare two or more companies' performances within the same sector. You also get a fair idea of estimating the returns on your investment over a given period.

The financial valuation of a company involves analysing its annual report. It helps an investor understand whether the stock price is overvalued, undervalued, or rightly valued. This information is of paramount importance while choosing to invest in stocks.

14

Michael Porter's Five Forces Framework for Industrial Analysis

One of the crucial steps in picking stocks is to analyse the industry to which the chosen company belongs. After all, the size of the fish is limited by the size of the pond. So, the profits of a company depend on its own growth as well as the growth of the industry.

This is what Michael Porter's Five Forces model was designed to do: Analyse industries.

The Five Forces model is an analytical tool to understand the economic viability of a company concerning its industry. It was designed by Michael Porter in 1979, and its relevance exists till date. This model helps you analyse the weaknesses and the strengths of various industries and serves as a tool to pick the right companies while choosing to invest in stocks.

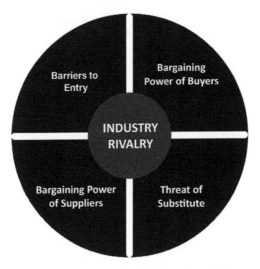

The five forces in Michael Porter's model

Porter's model is used to formulate the right strategies to support the long-term sustainability of businesses.

The success of a business in an industry is dependent on the following five factors:

1. Barriers to entry
2. Bargaining power of suppliers
3. Bargaining power of buyers
4. Threat of substitutes
5. Industry rivalry

With the help of these forces, a company can clearly understand its competitive stand in a particular industry. Now, let's dig deeper.

Barriers to Entry

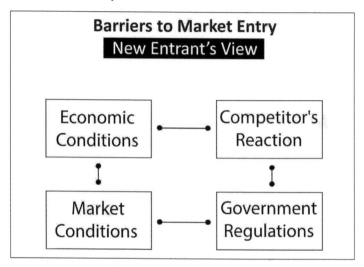

Barriers to entry for a company

Barriers to entry are challenges that companies face in entering a new business market. These challenges comprise the parameters shown in the figure above.

When many entrants enter a trade, the competition rises, and the profit share of each of the entrants gets smaller. Hence, the existing players ensure that the barriers to entry for their industry are high enough to stop the entry of many new players.

Here is a list of questions to help you gauge how easy it is for new entrants to enter an industry.

- How much capital is needed to start the business? It is easier to enter a new market when the amount of capital needed to start a new business is low.

- What are the government regulations and legal barriers, like trademarks, copyrights, etc., for entering the business? If the government regulations are not very rigid, many new entrants to an industry can be expected.
- How many brands are there in the market? What is the brand power or the reputation of the existing brands?
- How many products of the same category exist?
- What kind of access is provided to the suppliers and distributors?
- How easy is it to achieve economies of scale?
- What is the loss of exiting from the business?

An interesting example of a high barrier to entry is Facebook, which is the leader with a dominant market share in the social media industry. Due to its excellent network, it is difficult for new players to enter the industry.

Another example is civil explosive manufacturing units, which pose a stiff barrier to new entrants. The government is stringent in issuing licences to manufacture explosives, and so the existing players earn enormous profits.

A smart investor looks for industries with less scope of new entrants, as this suggests more significant profit shares for the existing players.

Bargaining Power of Suppliers

The bargaining power of suppliers refers to the negotiating power that suppliers have to impose their terms and conditions on the buyers. If the suppliers have good bargaining power, they sell the resources at higher prices than expected, or they may even sell raw materials of inferior quality.

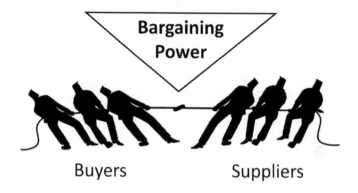

In either case, the profit margins of the buyers suffer badly, which, in turn, negatively affects the investors' profits.

So, to gauge the bargaining power of suppliers, the following concerns must be addressed:

- How many suppliers exist in the market?
- What is the size of the top 10 suppliers of the industry?
- What is the industry norm for order size for each supply?
- What is the cost of the closest substitutes available?
- Are the buyers capable of backward integration with suppliers? If yes, then are there plenty of such buyers or just a handful of them?

A real-life example of the high bargaining power of suppliers is that of Intel. Intel holds the majority of the market share to manufacture processors for laptops and desktop computers. It wouldn't be wrong to say that it is one of the biggest suppliers of processors. So, laptop manufacturers like HP, Apple, Dell, etc. have to purchase processors at the prices defined by Intel.

On the other hand, an example of the low bargaining power of suppliers is with respect to Indian Railways, which is owned by the public sector in India. Even though many companies manufacture wagons, the railways are the only buyers. Thus, the suppliers cannot dictate their pricing terms to the railways, and they end up earning low-profit margins.

Remember, the suppliers have a strong bargaining power when:

- The number of suppliers is less than the number of buyers.
- The resources are scarce.
- The alternatives or substitutes for the raw materials are limited.
- The suppliers dominate in the industry and may consider forward integration with dealers.

Low bargaining power of suppliers allows companies to work on their own terms, inviting better profits for investors in those companies.

Bargaining Power of Buyers

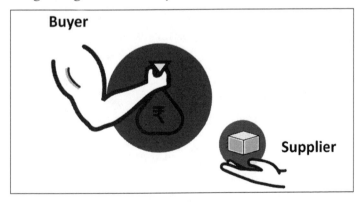

The bargaining power of buyers refers to the negotiating power that buyers have to impose their terms and conditions on the suppliers. The buyers use their power to demand high-quality products, lower prices, and better customer support.

Remember, the buyers have a strong bargaining power when:

- The quantity of raw material purchased is enormous.
- The number of buyers is limited.
- There are plenty of suppliers available.
- The buyers can integrate with suppliers.
- There are many substitutes for raw materials.
- The market is highly price sensitive.

A real-life example of the low bargaining power of buyers is that of the pharma sector in India. In the case of pharma or FMCG companies, all 130 crore Indians use their products. Hence, owing to a vast customer base, the companies manage to make huge profits consistently, even when their customers switch to competitors' products. Therefore, the bargaining power of customers, in this case, is very low.

The bargaining power of buyers must be low so that they cannot dominate the companies, which otherwise would hit the profits of the investors in those companies.

Threat of Substitutes

The threat of substitutes arises when buyers have the choice to settle conveniently with an alternative without spending much more. For example, tea and coffee are highly compatible substitutes; if one is not available, the buyer happily settles for the other.

Coffee   **Tea**

So, to gauge the threat of substitutes, you must figure out the following:

- How many substitutes exist in the market?
- What is the cost incurred by the buyer in switching to a substitute?
- How are the other substitutes performing relative to the chosen product?

A real-life example of a high threat of substitutes is the 'beer and wine' industry, which is part of the larger beverage industry. Another example of an industry with a high threat of substitutes is 'natural gas and petroleum.'

The threat of substitutes must be low for companies to make good profits, which acts in the investor's favour.

Industry Rivalry

The competitive rivalry of any industry depends on how profitable or competitive the industry is.

Having too much competition can deal a severe blow to your business. Hence, to stay safe, try to find out the following:

- How many competitors exist in the market?
- What is the current size of the industry?
- What is the rate at which the industry is growing?
- What is the size of the existing top, medium, and lowest competitors?
- Are there any threats of horizontal integration?
- What is the intensity of promotional campaigns and advertisements done to sell the products?

Competitors' rivalry in an industry must always be low to allow companies to make a bigger share of profits, which favours investors.

These are some of the basic questions you should ask to get a fair idea about the industry and its current valuations as well as expected valuations in the future. It is not necessary to find answers to all the questions, but answering even a handful from each category can give you a fair understanding of the industry.

How to Use Porter's Model to Your Advantage?

To use Porter's model to your advantage, follow these three basic steps:

Step 1: Gather Information

This is the most critical step in this model. The more you research about the industry, the more you get to learn about it. Your most important decision-making tool for stock investment is your knowledge, so try to acquire as much knowledge as possible.

Step 2: Analyse the Information

Once you have gathered all the data, you have to analyse it by posing the questions that we have just learnt.

Step 3: Make Strategies

The information and analysis you have drawn so far will help you come up with the right strategies. Here are a few examples of how this information will help you to formulate these strategies:

- If there are too many players or competitors in the market, it indicates the industry is at a slow growth rate. The industry is heading towards saturation with not much scope of survival for new entrants unless there is strong product differentiation.
- If the suppliers are dominant, then the profit margins are highly constrained and are connected to the suppliers' policies. The petroleum industry is an example since the fuel prices are determined by cartels such as OPEC.
- If the entry cost is too high, the stakes or the risk of taking up the business will also be very high. For example— opening a posh hotel, opening a car showroom, or a branded jewellery showroom. In such cases, you need to look at the industry's growth, demand for products, existing players, nature of the industry, etc.

The Key Takeaways from Porter's Model

Porter's Five Forces model is a superb tool to analyse the market, but it has its limitations, which are as follows: (from Porter, M.E., 2008, 'The Five Competitive Forces That Shape Strategy', *Harvard Business Review*)

- Porter's tool works out differently for different industries. The results and interpretations can even vary for similar industries. So, every sector needs to be studied thoroughly before jumping to any conclusions.
- This model has its limitations, which is why it is suggested that you also use other analytical tools, like SWOT analysis, Value Chain Analysis, or PEST analysis.
- This model works best when used for the industry and not for a single company.
- You must use this model when there are at least three competitors in the industry.
- You must also take a look at the government's input in the recent past in the chosen industry.
- While analysing any sector, you must evaluate the stages of the life cycle of the industry. The early stages of growth are a bit more challenging and need to be analysed accordingly.
- You must try to figure out if the industry is changing for good, for bad, or is stagnant to be assured of your investment.

Applying Porter's Five Forces Model to the Airline Industry

So far, we have discussed Porter's Five Forces model, which helps in detailed industry analysis. Now, we will apply the model to the airline industry.

Barriers to Entry: High

It is not easy for a new player to enter the airline industry, because of:

- Strict government regulations
- Immense capital investment
- High gestation period

These three challenges provide a definite competitive advantage to the existing players to dominate the airline industry and limit the entry of new players.

Bargaining Power of Suppliers: Very High

An aircraft is built on two major parts. One is the aircraft itself, and the other is its jet engine. There are mainly two companies that are into commercial aircraft manufacturing, namely Airbus and Boeing.

These two companies are the major suppliers of aircraft, and they cater to hundreds of airlines across the world. Thus, they have high negotiating powers, and the buyers are forced to pay the price that these suppliers quote.

Similarly, there are mainly three commercial jet engine manufacturers in the world. And again, because of their monopoly, they enjoy a high bargaining power.

Bargaining Power of Buyers: High

What do we look for when buying air tickets? Do we look for a specific brand? Will you pay a higher price just to travel on your preferred airline? Of course not! We will instead buy the cheapest available ticket. Thus, to sell the seats, the airlines keep their ticket cost low to grab as many customers as possible. These companies do not enjoy pricing power at all.

Let's use another example to bring a fresh perspective to this analysis. Paracetamol is a widely used drug that is manufactured by almost every pharma company. But whenever we have a fever or pain, we go out to buy Crocin, even when cheaper substitutes are readily available. And in this case, we don't mind paying extra for Crocin because it doesn't affect our wallet to a large extent (even though it is far costlier). But when it comes to airlines, we are not willing to pay even 10 per cent more for a ticket, as that 10 per cent premium payment substantially affects our wallets.

Therefore, the airlines do not have any power to decide air ticket fares, and there is no brand loyalty in this industry. This is precisely the reason why Indigo is currently the only successful operator, as it chooses to operate at a lower cost compared to its competitors.

Threat of Substitutes: Medium

The closest substitute to the airline industry can only be the railways. In some developed countries, the railways and airlines compete to grab more customers, because the railways run on high-speed networks and offer the same level of comfort as that of air travel. But in India, the situation is very different. The railways offer superb affordability at the cost of prolonged travel times, but the airlines provide quick transportation at the expense of hiked prices. So, there is a clear boundary between the two modes of travel that are mutually exclusive and not treated as substitutes.

But the situation is set to change in the coming years with the introduction of more and more high-speed rail corridors. As more routes are mapped by high-speed trains, the airlines will find it increasingly tough to compete.

Industry Rivalry: Medium

Due to cut-throat competition in the industry, many airlines have failed in the past and have been forced to shut operations or merge with more significant players.

Presently, we have the following players in India:

- Indigo
- Spice Jet
- Air India
- Go Air

- Vistara
- Air Asia
- Other Regional Players

These airlines fight tooth and nail to get the best high-traffic time slots, frequently travelled routes, etc. Even the premium airline players in India like Vistara and Air India have to fight with low-cost operators on competitive pricing.

I hope this quick analysis has shown you how to use Porter's Five Forces model to analyse any industry.

15

What's the Business Capable of?

I am sure you have noticed that if a company makes good money, it is soon surrounded by plenty of competitors. Eventually, the profit margin of the company suffers as the profits get divided amongst all the competitors. But there are certain companies like Apple, Britannia, Zydus Wellness, etc., that are still going strong despite a lot of competition. How do these companies manage to stay strong? It is because of a strong competitive advantage.

Business analysis helps us identify any competitive advantage that a company has over its peers. The differentiating factors could be patents, brands, location, cost advantages, etc. These traits provide a company with a strong shield to compete with others. In financial terminology, the competitive advantage is often referred to as an economic moat.

Economic Moat: The 'Differentiator'

In the words of Warren Buffett, an economic moat is a company's ability to maintain a competitive advantage over its competitors.

In simple words, the moat is a competitive advantage with which a company runs its business successfully.

An economic moat refers to a unique service or product that enables a company to create a strong brand value for a long period. As soon as a company launches a new idea in the market, the competition increases because of high margins. This is where economic moats come into the picture and provide a tremendous competitive advantage to such businesses that face fierce competition.

But how does knowing the moat of a company help in stock investment?

Generally, to know how good a company is, you look at its previous financial track record. But the past track record cannot give you complete assurance of its future. Thus, moats help you understand how strongly the company will be able to compete in the future. And by understanding the moat, you can place your best bets on the most promising companies.

How can you ascertain if the moat is sustainable?

Of course, the moats are susceptible to erosion with time. The only way to assess if moats remain sustainable is if a company follows a strong business model that does not get affected in the longer run.

Different Types of Moats to Look for in a Company

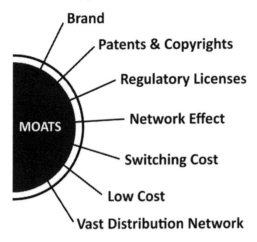

There are various types of moats to look for in a company, which are as follows.

1. *Brands:* You may have noticed that you ask for Crocin instead of paracetamol tablets when you visit a medicine shop. Or you often say Maggi instead of instant noodles when you visit a kirana store. Such strong brands often become a part of our routine life and are reflected in our vocabulary.

    Here, as you can see, the product branding is so powerful that it overshadows all the product variants available in the market. And this is to such an extent that those variants are also bought in that product's name. So, companies manufacturing Crocin and Maggi have a strong economic moat to sustain.

2. *Regulatory licences:* Regulatory licences also serve as an economic moat for several companies. For example, credit

rating agencies, NSE, BSE, etc. have enjoyed a long-standing monopoly in the market. Such companies have the edge over others because they are licensed to perform certain activities that others are not.

2. *Patents and copyrights:* Patent refers to an intellectual property right given to an entity for a limited period to retain exclusive rights to manufacturing, selling, or using an innovative product or service. Patents are given to provide an exclusive opportunity to the inventor to enjoy full commercial benefits for a limited period.

    For instance, the pharma industry thrives and survives on drug patents. A patent is one of the reasons why certain medicines are so expensive, as they are protected under patent rights.

3. *Network effect:* A few companies do exceptionally well because their products have an extensive network of users, which is referred to as the network effect. In such cases, the value of a product or service increases with the increase in the number of users.

    For example, everyone uses MS Office because everyone else is using it.

    Another example is Facebook—the more the number of users, the better the value of the social media platform. People prefer to stay on Facebook because they know that their family and friends are available on it. Another famous example is WhatsApp—you prefer it over other chat apps like WeChat because you find all your friends there.

4. *Switching cost:* This serves as an economic moat for those products where the time, cost, and inconvenience of changing to a competitor's product is too high, and so customers prefer sticking to the same product. For

example, people with an Airtel phone number would stick to it even if they don't find Airtel's services satisfactory. It is because switching would mean redistributing a new number to all contacts, which is cumbersome and time-consuming. Thankfully, mobile number portability has eradicated switching cost.

Another example is your bank account. It is difficult to switch your salary or savings account to different banks as all services linked to your account get disrupted, and you have to put in a lot of effort to realign them to your new account.

On the contrary, if you have a loyalty card of Big Bazaar and you learn that DMart has become cheaper, then you will immediately switch to DMart. This is because, in this case, there are no ties of any sort as a customer.

5. *Low cost:* Cost acts as an economic moat when the manufacturing cost of the product is significantly low. For example, many cement industries establish their plants near lime resources to minimize the cost of sourcing the raw material and the cost of distribution of the finished product. So, for cement companies, what matters is the availability of quality products at lower prices. Of course, product differentiation is minimum in such cases. Some other examples of this category of products are oil, power, and iron.

6. *Vast distribution network:* A vast distribution network serves as an economic moat when the extensive network helps the company to replenish its stock instantly to ensure that the product is always available on the shelf.

Let's consider an example. Ravi resided in a small town called Saharanpur. He wanted to buy a car. Ravi was quite excited about the launch of MG Hector and wanted to purchase one. But since there wasn't any MG dealership in his town, he had to settle for a Maruti Suzuki Vitara Brezza.

Many small companies with remarkable products die out eventually as their products never reach the end-users on time. It shows that they are left behind by the companies that have a vast distribution network as an economic moat. On the contrary, companies like Pepsi, Coca-Cola, HUL, and P&G dominate the market due to their strong distribution network.

Thus, it is crucial to analyse a business completely before investing in it. As an investor, you must not rely on the short-term profits of a company but must look at its long-term viability.

Customer Stickiness

Everyone enjoys going out on dinner outings with family or friends, but do you visit the same restaurant every week? Of course not! We look forward to a new change in every outing. So, there is always a hunt for new places to visit every weekend.

Now think about these products:

- Tata Salt
- Amul Butter
- Nescafé
- Crocin

Can you recollect the last time you used these products? And since when have you been using these products? Why don't we try any other paracetamol tablet apart from Crocin or Calpol (which, by the way, are manufactured by the same company)? Why don't we buy any salt other than Tata Salt?

The reason is simple—these products are habit-based; they derive their value from consistency and not novelty. Products that are valued for their consistency, such as Coke, Nescafé, Lays, Colgate, etc., are far more successful bets than products that rely on providing a unique experience or the novelty factor. For example, clothes represent a category in which fashion changes quickly as everyone wants to look different. Hence, these companies incur huge R&D costs to bring in the latest fashion trends. In their quest to satiate the fashion longings of their target customers, the garment companies also end up with a huge dead inventory.

Therefore, we see this huge competition and dozens of companies struggling in the denim, shirts, and trousers segment. No one is a clear winner; no one is making huge money. On the other hand, you don't look for fashion or innovation in innerwear; the essential factor is the comfort and experience with the brand. So, a Jockey suits you perfectly and sells like hotcakes. And with this, you've learnt the first rule for identifying customer stickiness, which is:

Rule 1: Look for companies with products that sell because of customer habits and consistency.

Now, take a look at the following questions:

- Will you buy gold from a jeweller who is not reliable? *No.*
- Will you buy a T-shirt from a shop owner you don't know? *Maybe.*

Why was the answer different for the two questions? Two reasons:

1. Value or price of the product
2. Importance of the product

If the product you are buying is cheap and possible inferior quality of the product won't cause any harm, then you won't be fussy about the product quality. But if the product is costly, you will think twice before experimenting with a new brand or seller.

Remember that every time, the product doesn't have to be costly. You have to be careful before buying it. After all, a paracetamol tablet costs less than one rupee. But we are very careful about its quality and brand because its inferior quality might cause a lot of harm to you.

This is also the reason why car companies are struggling to snatch market share from Maruti. Maruti is a trusted brand;

no one wants to experiment with their money by buying a car from a company other than Maruti. Since we incur a huge cost in buying a car, we tend to play safe and stick to the tried and tested brand. And this calls for the second rule, which is:

Rule 2: Look for brands that sell because of their perceived or actual superior quality and trust.

Apart from this, what else should you look for?

Look for products or services that have a large user base and high switching costs. For example, HDFC Bank has a vast user base. The bank has a close relationship with its clients because of the up-selling and cross-selling of its products. A typical HDFC Bank customer will probably have the following relationships with the bank:

- Savings account (own and family)
- Current account (for business owners)
- Credit card
- Bank locker
- Life insurance
- Mutual funds
- Home/car loan

Imagine a customer who has availed so many products or services of HDFC Bank. Do you think he will switch because some other bank on the block is offering 1 per cent higher interest? He will think of all the complexities and paperwork involved and will most likely choose to stick to HDFC.

So, we can be sure that HDFC Bank will show stable earnings for the foreseeable future, making companies like these an excellent option to invest in. This helps us in formulating the third rule, which is:

Rule 3: Look for companies with a large customer base along with high switching costs.

In a nutshell, you must look for companies that:

1. Have habit-forming products or services
2. Are valued because of the consistent consumer experience they provide
3. Enjoy huge goodwill and trust
4. Have a large and 'sticky' consumer base

Basically, these three rules teach us to hunt for companies that have the advantage of customer stickiness to them. If customers keep returning to buy the products or services of the company, it ensures regular earnings for the company, which assures your growth as an investor.

Forecasting Growth

Forecasting the growth of a company is a regular practice used by investors. In the long run, the price of shares rises roughly in tandem with the increase in profits.

Here are a few things the average stock market investor tries to predict regularly:

- Whether the market will rise or fall tomorrow.
- Whether company ABC's share price will rise tomorrow.
- Whether interest rates will rise.
- Whether inflation will fall, etc.

We need to understand that trying to answer such questions is meaningless, and they don't help in better stock choices at all. Newspapers often sell such information as financial noise to keep us hooked. And in the words of Peter Bernstein, 'Forecasts create the mirage that the future is knowable.'

> *'There are two kinds of forecasters: Those who don't know, and those who don't know they don't know.'*
>   —Economist John Kenneth Galbraith

Forecasting is not just seen in stocks. You can see television experts trying to predict the quarterly earnings of every stock on earth. Experts try to forecast the future of everything—GDP, weather, even the Third World War! But have you wondered why people are interested in predicting everything around them? Forecasting, if it turns out to be true, increases the smartness quotient of the forecaster; it is a skill that gives them an immense fan following. So, people predict the future to gain name and fame.

I see analysts trying to predict the estimated earnings for the next five years of hundreds of companies. What's worse, they seem to precisely know how much Company X will earn after five years. We can still relate to this if they give a range of expected earnings, but then a range won't make them look smart, so they will provide you with an exact figure up to multiple decimal points.

For example, a typical research report will tell you that Company X earned Rs 100 crore in 2017, and its expected earnings in the year 2022 will be Rs 137.55 crore! This is how sure these research analysts are about the earnings five years down the line! So, this means that these guys are a bunch of geniuses, doesn't it?

Let's compare this to what Warren Buffett has to say about forecasting revenues. He claims that he doesn't even know what his own company will earn the next month, so forget about predicting figures five years hence. Here is the greatest investor on earth confessing that earnings are unpredictable, even if it's his own company. But these so-called analysts will confidently predict the next 100 years' earnings if they are paid to do it. Now you are smart enough to understand whether you should rely on predictions or not.

In the stock market, not all predictions are bad. But the important thing is to differentiate the predictable from the unpredictable.

Here are some examples showing what is predictable and what is not.

1. Will we develop a time machine in the next 50 years? *Unpredictable.*
2. Will we need food and water to survive after 20 years? *Predictable.*
3. Will we start a civilization on Mars? *Unpredictable.*
4. Will people travel more by air in the next five years? *Predictable.*

So, the first step is to segregate the predictable from the unpredictable. The second step is to segregate between the 'hard to predict' and 'easy to predict' questions. Here is an example:

1. Will people travel more by air in the next 10 years?
   - Predictable – Yes

2. Will India invest in constructing more airports?
    *   Easy to predict – Yes

3. How many new airports will come up in the next 10 years?
    *   Hard to predict

So, your learning is: Invest based on 'easy to predict' questions.

You must invest in stocks based on answers to questions that are easy to predict. Easy-to-predict things do not require a precise forecast, as the more specific your assumption is, the higher is the risk of it going wrong.

For example, if I were to ask you, 'Will you invest in Zydus Wellness?', then your answer must depend on the following questions:

1. Do you think people will become more diet-conscious?
2. Do you think the Sugar Free brand has a huge brand recall?

If the answer to these two questions is yes, you can further analyse Zydus as an investment option. So, the right investment strategy requires you to make generalized and not specific assumptions.

Now let's take another example. 'Will you invest in a company that makes medicines for blood cancer patients?' Let's figure out how to answer this.

1. Do you think the occurrence of blood cancer will rise?
2. Do you think there will be no cure for blood cancer?

3. Do you think this company will remain a competitive manufacturer of blood cancer drugs?

As you can see, the answers to these questions are much harder to forecast. Such investing decisions, based on hard-to-predict responses, should be avoided.

16

Management Analysis

For any company to succeed, it is essential for it to have the right set of top officials to formulate the right strategies for the business. The top management of the company manages the entire business operations. They are required to take the crucial decisions of the company, like funds diversification, product differentiation, business expansion, etc. The CEOs are the key drivers behind charting a business' course to success.

The example of Apple Inc. best shows the importance of the management of the company. Steve Jobs had worked with Apple for some time; then he quit Apple and re-joined it after a few years. Here is how his presence and absence impacted the company.

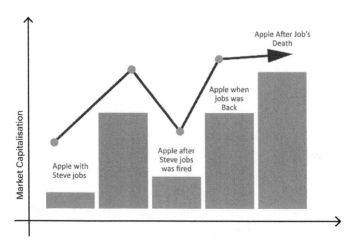

Apple's performance with and without Steve Jobs

From the graph, it is clear that Apple performed at its best when Steve Jobs was running it, and the company clearly struggled in his absence.

In India, Ratan Tata, Aditya Puri, Uday Kotak, Azim Premji, Adi Godrej, etc., have been the key people behind businesses reaching the pinnacle of success. This is the power of efficient management!

The following step-by-step guide will help you evaluate the management of any company.

Evaluate Company Policies

Strong management is always the backbone of the company. It is not that the employees are unnecessary; of course, they are equally important, but it is the management that steers the business and ensures that it sails through a safe ride.

The first and foremost thing to look for is the company's policies for shareholders and its employees. This is to check how strong the management of a company is. Here is the checklist:

- Any company that talks only favourably about its policies, profits, and current happenings raises suspicion and calls for an alert. No business was, is, or will be run perfectly at all times.
- Every business will go through its phases of growth, maturity, and decline, and hence, the investors must be informed about the challenges and the repercussions of the same openly.

Check the Vision and Mission of the Company

The vision and the mission of the company define the long-term and short-term goals of the company, respectively. The top officials of the company make the vision and the mission of the company.

So, you must consider the following points while evaluating a company for investment:

- Is the short-term mission of the company in line with its long-term vision?
- What are the steps being taken by the top management to support the vision of the company?
- Are there any programmes or events being held to promote the vision of the organization?

How Does the Management Allocate Excess Funds?

Running a business well, and earning profits from it form just one part of the story. How the earned benefits are used to grow the business further is what decides the longevity or the survival of the business.

The excess funds of a business are represented by free cash flow (FCF), which is the actual cash inflow of the company after incurring all operating as well as capital expenditures.

Here are some of the ways in which the management uses its FCF.

- Reinvest the FCF back into the business to develop the business further.
- Pay good dividends to shareholders.
- Acquire new companies.
- Buy back the stocks of its own company.

All these practices act in favour of the company and increase its business value in the longer run.

Do you know that allocating funds wisely is a crucial parameter for a business' success?

Capital allocation is a big responsibility that must be taken up by a top official of a company to get the best results. The performance of each CEO varies and depends on their competencies and capabilities. The best way to allow any CEO to perform at their best is to segregate operational and capital allocation job roles.

Two live examples of this are Warren Buffett of Berkshire Hathaway and Ajay Piramal of Piramal Enterprises. These two entrepreneurs only take care of the capital allocation of the business, which is why they have been able to take their businesses to new heights by making smart investment choices.

Another example is that of Henry Singleton, who has been much applauded for his excellent investment decisions in the past and has been ranked as the best investor by Warren Buffett. So, if a company has somebody solely responsible for allocating capital, it indicates a good business practice.

Check How the Company Compensates the Top Management

This point has been discussed in detail in the chapter 'A Closer Look at the Annual Report'.

Watch Out If You See Top Officials Announcing Stock Prices Every Quarter!

It is great for an investor to hear the stock price valuation straight from the horse's mouth. However, if the top management often takes the lead in predicting the quarterly stock valuation, then it indicates that the management is paying way too much heed to short-term goals.

This often misleads serious investors, who keep themselves away from short-term price fluctuations of the stocks. Because the management itself is announcing the stock prices, it shows that the management believes a lot in short-term price fluctuations of the stocks.

You must avoid such companies, as their vision gets way too narrow to survive in the longer run.

Is the Company Reasonably Spending All the Hard-Earned Money?

When you hear of too many swanky offices of a company coming up in different parts of cities, then it must raise your eyebrows.

Of course, providing employee comfort and benefits in terms of a good work environment is essential, but companies sometimes lose sight of the bigger picture by investing in just one aspect of business development. State-of-the-art offices must be developed only after investing in key business development activities to help the business thrive.

Does the Company Share the Bad News Openly?

You will find companies talking about the good events in the company. But you will seldom come across companies that are equally eager and open to sharing the bad news. An example to substantiate this point is as follows.

Suppose the sales of a company have grown from Rs 10 crore to Rs 12 crore, and the net profit has gone down from Rs 10 crore to 8 crore.

How do you think this company must report these figures?

The company must state that *the sales grew by Rs 2 crore, which is 20 per cent of the growth rate, but the net profit has declined by Rs 2 crore.*

This is how a company must report the real picture to its shareholders in newsletters or on the website to help them understand where the business is currently. But what you see most companies reporting is as follows:

Sales growth by 20 per cent, net profit is at Rs 8 crore.

This very subtly indicates the intent of the top management, i.e., to misrepresent/conceal facts in order to be in the good books of investors. Smart investors will understand these cues and will know the real face of the management of this company.

Is the Management a Trendsetter or a Trend Follower?

When a company is a part of any billion-dollar industry, then it is quite natural to follow the competitors, but if the management follows a trend only to prove itself better than the lot, then an investor needs to be watchful.

It is often seen that when a company acquires a competitor, it immediately becomes news, which portrays the company as a powerful player in the industry. This builds a lot of insecurities among other competitors who want to prove their worth as well. And hence, they too get into an acquisition without analysing their moves.

Here are some interesting examples from the past.

1. Tata Steel acquiring Corus was big news and an equally big disaster as well!
2. Hindalco acquiring Novelis was, again, a huge mistake.

One of the smart ways to check whether there was merit behind an acquisition or it was only to match the competitors is to see if the top officials of the company are bragging about such mergers and acquisitions or not. Usually, the CEOs brag about such acquisitions when they want to satisfy their ego.

Check Tenure of Association of Top Management with the Company

If you have watched somebody for an extended period, it becomes easy to predict his performance in the future as well. On the contrary, it gets difficult to judge somebody who has started being in the public eye only recently, as his performance has not been witnessed yet.

So, look for a company whose top management has been around for at least a decade to prove their worth. In such cases, the consistent positive performances of senior officials reassure us about their interests and capabilities, which are the ultimate keys to success.

Is the Company a Flat Organization, or Does It Follow the Bureaucratic Culture?

Though bureaucracy is highly discouraged, many public sector undertakings and some big corporations are bureaucratic in approach.

Bureaucracy involves many levels or layers of management and follows the top-down control approach. Bureaucratic organizations are rigid, as they lack the creativity and flexibility of operating in an organization. Such practices indicate poor management policies for the organization.

For example, the State Bank of India (SBI) is highly bureaucratic and invites red-tapism, resulting in delayed work. Because of this, it has lost many opportunities that came in its way. Though SBI is growing at a fast pace, it would have already become much bigger had it only avoided the bureaucratic approach.

HDFC Bank, on the other hand, is a flat banking organization with much quicker responses due to the absence of bureaucracy. Hence, it could touch new heights of success in no time.

Does the Company Have Clear Communication?

Clear and straightforward communication must be visible in the annual reports of the company. These reports must show that the management takes responsibility for all its actions. The intent of the management can also be gauged by the following communications:

Newsletters given to shareholders: You must read all the past newsletters that were circulated by the company to its shareholders. These newsletters disclose critical information like:

a. What is the aim of running the business?
b. What is the current financial health of the company?
c. What led to the critical decisions in the recent past?
d. What are the business prospects in the near future?
e. What are the challenges faced by the company in meeting its targets, and how does the management intend to resolve them?

Conference call letters: Often, conferences discuss recent issues in a long meeting, where all the shareholders of the company are present. Such discussions are noted down in the minutes of the meeting to keep as a record for future references.

You must go through all transcripts of past conferences, which will give you a reasonably good idea about how openly the company has been talking about its challenges. You may come across statements by the management like, 'We will not be able to disclose all the information as we do not let our competitors know about our strategies in the interest of the business.' Such statements signal a red alert, as a company must look at outperforming its competitors by any means rather than focusing on hiding information from its investors.

Is the CEO Very Media-Friendly?

If you find the top-most official of the company appearing a lot on media channels, then he is somebody who gets carried away by the name and fame of the business. Such people are often flamboyant, have a lot of charisma, show aggressive salesmanship, and boast a lot about their accomplishments. Watch out for such CEOs and stay away from companies that employ these overpriced officials to run the show!

Often, in the quest of becoming a showstopper, such people lose the battle terribly!

How Is the Top Management Hired?

This is yet another thought-provoking question when it comes to analysing the managing machinery of a company. In some companies, the family members are, by default, made the top management of the company, whereas, in many others, the right people are placed in the right positions.

Although the former situation is favourable as the owners will act in the company's best interests, the family members must not hold all top positions. Moreover, it is essential to see if the family members are the right fit for strategic decision-making, as they will be the key drivers of the business.

Though there is nothing right or wrong here, and the idea to learn about the hiring policies is only to see how fair the company is in its dealings, it would be right to say that there must be a healthy mix of insiders and outsiders for interest and innovation to work together in the company's best interest.

Assure Yourself That the Management Is Trustworthy

Whether the management is trustworthy or not can be ascertained by figuring out the answers to the following questions:

- Does the management follow ethical practices like integrity?
- Does the management openly disclose the strengths and weaknesses of the company?
- Does the management reinvest the profits, raise the equity holders' dividends or hoard the money?
- Has the company made any acquisitions in the past, and have they paid off?
- Has the top management been reinvesting in its stocks?
- Does the management hold a good percentage of shares in its name? It shows the trust the management has in its own company as it is ready to bear both hefty profits and losses equally.

17

A Closer Look at the Annual Report

Analysing a Company

When you want to buy a car, you go around the market searching for the best brand and model for yourself. You check out different brands to compare their mileage, power, durability, performance, etc. After all this necessary groundwork, you decide on the best one to buy.

Similarly, before investing in any company, you have to understand its annual report, which indicates the true financial health of the company.

So, let's get started with the real basics of analysing the financial health of a company.

What Is an Annual Report?

The annual report of a company is a snapshot of its business activities of the preceding year. At the end of every financial year, every company publishes its annual report on its website.

The annual report is sent to the shareholders of the company every year.

Here are the qualitative and quantitative parameters to look for while reading an annual report.

Design and Tone of the Report

The design and tone of the annual report must be easy to understand for lay investors. The purpose of publishing an annual report is to share and disclose key information to the shareholders and other prospective investors. However, a few companies treat the annual report as a part of the company's public relations activities to woo existing and potential shareholders and attract investment in the company.

Do you know that some companies act smart by twisting the tone and design of the report? They use excessively bright colours and pictures to make it look attractive, and this misleads the readers by overshadowing important information.

However, the opposite also exists. One such example would be Goodyear India, which is a reputed brand and gives a truly straightforward annual report. Goodyear India puts just three to four colourful pages at the beginning, which share the details of the company's top management, and soon after, it gets straight to the subject.

A snapshot of an annual report of Goodyear

Highlighted Graphs and Diagrams

As an investor, when you sit down to read the annual report of a company, you must look at the increase in earnings per share or EPS.

Some companies fill pages with graphs containing sales revenue, earnings, etc., but they will hardly mention the EPS. But what good is the company if it cannot tell its current shareholders or potential shareholders about their EPS?

Management Discussion and Analysis

In this section, you will get the following insights:

- How does the management perceive the present position of the company in the market?
- What is the management's feeling about the future of the company?
- What business activities are planned for the future?

Here, the company must attempt to resolve investors' dilemmas and the risk associated with investing in the company.

But, if after reading through this section, you feel that you did not understand the information given, then you can be sure that the management intended it that way. At times, the reports are loaded with buzzwords such as 'synergy,' 'strategic,' etc., only to fill up space.

Management Remuneration

Compensation acts as an excellent means of motivation for one and all, including the CEO. In the organization, the CEO is undoubtedly the highest earner, which is, of course, well deserved! If the CEO is compensated in proportion to earned profits, his interest is always maintained in the company. And, most importantly, you must try to understand *how the top management of the company is compensated if the business is not doing well.*

For example, if a CEO owns stock worth Rs 5 crore and has an annual salary of Rs 1 crore, then he strives hard to ensure that the company grows. However, if the same CEO owns shares worth Rs 5 crore and is paid an annual salary of Rs 8 crore, then his interest may be restricted to performing within the boundaries defined by the job, rather than going the extra mile to grow the company. Thus, the interest of the CEO towards the company will be higher in the prior case than in the latter one.

Hence, the management of a company is considered the best when it continually increases its ownership in the company. *You can find these details on the BSE (formerly, Bombay Stock Exchange) website easily and see how much each management has invested in their own companies.*

Now, let us look at another situation where the company is owned and managed by a family. In such cases, the investor must check the quantum of salary and other forms of compensation that the management extracts from the company. Some promoters extract up to 10 per cent of the profits of the company in the form of salaries (10 per cent is the ceiling as per the Companies Act, 2013). A management that rewards itself excessively doesn't care about its shareholders.

Do you think it would be wise to invest in such companies? Of course not! Any increase in the management's remuneration should always be in proportion to the company's profits. If the performance of the company is deteriorating, but the management's compensation is increasing, it is a red flag indicating that such companies must be avoided.

Promoters' Shareholding

Promoters are the insiders of the company with the best knowledge of the business' operations. So, in case the promoters are increasing their shareholding, it can be considered a positive sign. It also signifies that they are optimistic about the company's growth and strategies.

On the other hand, a decrease in promoters' shareholding can be taken as a negative sign, and it may express their loss of faith in the company. Think about it. Will you sell your stake in the business that you have nurtured carefully if you see a huge potential for growth in the future?

Sometimes, promoters' shareholding decreases for some other reasons, for instance, planning for a new venture or a new plant, etc. However, if the promoters' shares are continuously decreasing without any clear reasons, then you may need to investigate further and take cautionary action.

For example, during the Satyam scandal, Ramalinga Raju's holdings were continuously decreasing. He sold shares worth more than Rs 4.4 crore in the period from 2001 to 2008. Those who were following the shareholding pattern of the promoters might have seen these signs indicating danger for the investors.

Warrants A warrant is an alternative given to the management to buy the shares of the company at a price lower than the market price. As an investor, your aim should be to check if an excessive number of warrants has been issued to the management. This is because excessive warrants can dilute the EPS for equity shareholders.

Related-Party Transaction

This refers to the transaction between the company and any entity or individual who is directly related to the directors or the management. Though these transactions are legal, there are still chances that they may affect shareholders' interest. Let's consider an example. XYZ Ltd and ABC Pvt. Ltd are two companies. Asha is the CEO of XYZ Ltd., and her husband Abhay holds a 40 per cent stake in ABC Pvt. Ltd. Suppose ABC Pvt. Ltd is in a bad financial position and no bank is giving loans to it, but XYZ Ltd decides to take credit on its name and then pass it on to ABC Pvt. Ltd. Then this will be called a related party transaction. Such transactions hurt the shareholder's profits.

18

Analysing Financial Statements

A company's annual report comprises the following three basic components that are referred to as financial statements:

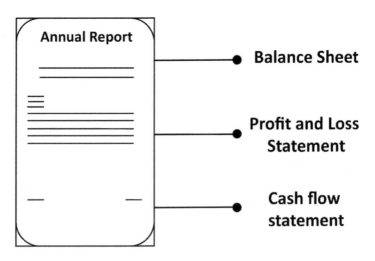

Let us explore each of these in detail.

Balance Sheet

In simple words, a balance sheet represents the company's financial position. It represents the total assets owned by the company and also discloses how these assets are financed—through debt or equity.

The balance sheet of a company is based on a fundamental accounting equation, which is as follows:

Capital (owner's funds) = Assets (possessions) - Liabilities (obligations)

Assets: Assets are resources that are owned by the company and are capable of generating future cash flows. Examples are cash, plants and machinery, furniture, etc. Depending upon the period of holding, assets can be classified as follows:

a. Current assets: These assets are held for less than one year and hence have higher liquidity—for example, cash and cash equivalents, stock, office supplies, short-term deposits.
b. Non-current assets (fixed assets): These assets are held by the company for more than one year and cannot be easily converted into cash—for example, land, building, furniture, etc.

Liabilities: Liabilities are monetary obligations of the entity that are required to be paid off. Some liabilities are generated in the day-to-day course of business, while some can be loans taken for a longer duration. Depending upon the payment period, liabilities can be classified as follows:

a. Current liabilities: These obligations have to be settled within a year—for example, payments to creditors, interest payable, short-term loans, etc.

b. Non-current liabilities: These obligations have to be settled after a year or more. They are important to determine the long-term solvency of the company. Non-current liabilities are normally loans taken by the company for projects, purchase of an asset, etc.

So, when we purchase machinery (an asset is increased), the cash reduces (an asset reduces). Thus, the asset remains unchanged, and hence, the equation remains satisfied. This is true for all transactions.

Statement of Profit and Loss

Profit and loss statements reflect the most important perspective of a company—its profitability. It is important to keep track of all the expenses incurred and all the revenues generated in the year. This statement reflects the three most important elements, as follows:

• Revenue generated during the year
• Expenses incurred during the year
• Net profit of the company

Revenue Generated during the Year

Every profit and loss statement starts with 'revenue from operations.' Revenue is different from profit and is the amount of sales generated during the year.

If you sell goods worth Rs 100 and your relevant costs are Rs 80, the net amount you earn = Rs 100 - Rs 80 = Rs 20.

In this case, revenue is Rs 100, and profit is Rs 20. So, we can say that the gross amount received for any transaction relating to the company's core business activity is called revenue from operations. 'Revenue' and 'sales' mean the same thing, and neither should be confused with profits.

Expenses

Expenses are incurred by the company for generating revenues. These can be for the purchase of raw materials, employee benefits, interest costs, etc. One major expense for the company is *depreciation, amortization, and impairment of an asset*. Let us understand each of these in brief.

Whenever a company buys any fixed assets, its benefit is expected to be enjoyed for more than one year. So, it is capitalized in the books. Capitalized means it is not treated as an expense and charged in the profit and loss (P/L) account, but is booked in the balance sheet as assets. Year by year, the value of assets is reduced, and a little part is booked as an expense in the name of depreciation of an asset.

For example, if a company has purchased a machine for Rs 10,000, and it is expected to provide benefits for 10 years, every year only Rs 1,000 is charged in the P/L account as depreciation to account for the wear and tear of the machine.

Similarly, if an intangible asset, such as trademark, copyright, goodwill, etc., is purchased by the company, it is 'amortized' every year.

And in case substantial damage has occurred to the machine during the year, the expense is booked as impairment of assets.

Net Profit

Net profit is the amount left with the company after all the expenses have been deducted. Net profit belongs to the shareholders of the company.

Cash Flow Statements

The cash flow statement is another important part of a financial statement, and it reflects liquidity. The liquidity of a company is how easily the company can convert its assets into cash to meet its short-term or current liabilities. So, even though a company owns many assets, a company can face liquidity issues if such assets cannot readily be converted into cash.

The cash flow statement tracks the flow of cash (inflow as well as outflow) from various sources throughout the year. It shows cash at the beginning of the year, additions and reductions in cash during the year, and the final balance at the end of the year.

All the three parts of financial statements—balance sheet, profit and loss statement, and cash flow statement—are important to analyse the true position of the company.

There may be a possibility that the company has a very attractive P/L statement during the year, but while going through the balance sheet, we find that the company is generating profits by selling off its fixed assets.

At other times, the P/L statement can also show losses during the year, but while going through the balance sheet, we realize that the company has created value for the shareholders by starting new businesses.

At times, it is also possible that both balance sheets and P/L statements represent huge turnover and high profits, but by looking into cash flow statements, we realize that the company is not able to recover money from its customers and is thus unable to pay back its loans on time.

Hence, we use various ratios that take elements from all three parts of financial statements and express a relationship between them. This brings a lot of clarity in understanding the real standing of a company. In this chapter, we will study various types of ratios, along with their computation and interpretation.

Going by convention, we generally compare ratios of various companies of the same industry, or ratios of the current financial findings of a company with its records to interpret the performance of the company.

Here, I would like to bring your attention to the fact that the right interpretation of ratios is far more important than being able to compute them. Of course, without computing them correctly, you will never be able to deduce the right findings. Nevertheless, the focus must be more on learning to interpret them correctly, which has been made easy in the following chapters.

As it is, the ratios often differ from analyst to analyst, so we will study some widely used ratios to make things easy. Depending upon the aspects measured by them, these ratios can be categorized as given in the following figure:

Various ratios used to analyse companies

Each ratio needs to be properly interpreted because that in turn, will provide you the clarity on how to use that particular ratio in understanding the performance of a company.

Let's understand the important ratios through a story.

Case Study: Kumar and His Business Idea

Kumar was a fresh MBA graduate, and his life goal was to set up a large-scale business. His father was an Indian Army officer who had just retired. Kumar had a business idea and wanted to incorporate his start-up, HeadLabs. The initial investment was not an issue because his father had received a decent post-retirement package, and better, he was open to helping his son pursue his dreams.

Inception of HeadLabs, Courtesy of Kumar's Dad

HeadLabs manufactures wireless headphones of medium range. They are not as costly as Bose and not as cheap as substandard brands available in the market head. They are positioned right in the middle.

First Year of Business

Kumar had an exciting first year of business. Following are the results that he got in April 2015.

Profit and loss statement of HeadLabs

	Amount (in Rs lakh)
Revenue from sales	80
Other income (commissions, dividends, etc.)	45
Total income	**125**
Less: Expenses	
Cost of raw materials	(25)
Rent	(10)
Administrative Expenses	(25)
Depreciation (wear and tear)	(10)
Interest	(5)
Other expenses (non-operating)	(5)
Profit before tax	**45**
Less: Tax at 30%	13.5
Net profit	**31.5**

Given next is the company's balance sheet.

Balance sheet of HeadLabs

	Amount (in Rs Lakh)
Share capital (money given by Kumar's father)	100
Reserve and surplus	31.5
Long-term borrowing (business loan)	43
Short-term borrowing (money borrowed from friends for short term)	25
Current liabilities	30.5
Total liabilities	**230**
Fixed assets	70
Capital work in progress	55
Investment	10
Cash	65
Inventory	10
Other current assets	20
Total assets	**230**

Now, suppose Kumar is your friend. He shows you this data and proposes a partnership for his company. Will you invest in the venture?

If you decided to invest straight away, you were wrong! And, if you rejected the proposal outright, you were still wrong! How is this possible? Well, the data is not sufficient to make an investment decision.

Now, you'll learn how to make an investment decision based on financial data.

Profitability Ratios

You would have seen a figure in the table on p. 137 (Profit and loss statement of HeadLabs) denoting profitability:

(Figures in Rs lakh)

Profit before tax	45
Less: Tax at 30%	13.5
Net Profit	31.5

Now, you get an option of investing with Bass-X, a competitor of Kumar's company that has reported a net profit of Rs 50 lakh. Which is the better option?

What did you choose? Was it Bass-X?

If you did, you're not alone. Most of the investors just look at the net profit and take a decision. But that's not the right way of doing it. The net profit of a company is an absolute figure. This tells us literally nothing! Even when you compare this number to another company's number, you won't get meaningful information.

You must be wondering how we can judge profitability. That's where profitability ratios come into play. The following are some of the profitability ratios.

Gross Profit Margin

This is a metric to evaluate the manufacturing efficiency of a company.

Let's go back to our example.

Net sales for HeadLabs in 2015, was Rs 80 lakh, and the total expenses related to manufacturing were Rs 25 lakh. So the gross profit of HeadLabs in 2015 was Rs 55 lakh.

Please do not confuse Gross Profit with Gross Profit Margin.

Gross profit is the difference between net sales and all manufacturing expenses, while gross profit margin is the proportion of gross profit to net sales.

In the case of HeadLabs, the gross profit margin is 68.75 per cent. Here's how we calculated it:

$$\text{Gross Profit Margin} = \frac{55}{80} \times 100$$

Now, consider this.

Suppose the average gross profit margin in this industry ranges from 50 to 60 per cent. Hence, HeadLabs has a competitive advantage over its peers, as indicated by its gross profit margin. This means that HeadLabs is able to manage its production cost better than its peers. It may be due to better inventory management, higher bargaining power, strong procurement policy, etc.

Thumb rule: The higher the gross profit margin, the higher will be the company's efficiency to generate profits.

Operating Profit Margin

Gross profit margin only shows manufacturing efficiency, but there are many other factors that play an important role in the functioning of a company. For example, HeadLabs would have spent on advertising and promotions to increase its sales. But this hasn't been considered in gross profit margin.

Some of the factors excluded in gross profit margin are expenses related to sales and administration like office rent, distribution expenses, promotional expenses, salaries of staff, etc.

Hence, Operating Profit Margin gives us the measure of the profit generated from business operations. It is the proportion of operating profit to net sales.

Operating profit = Gross profit - Operating expenses
So, Operating Profit = 55 - (10 + 25 + 10) = Rs 10 lakh

Hence, for HeadLabs, the operating profit margin is as follows:

$$\text{Operating Profit Margin} = \frac{10}{80} \times 100 = 12.5\%$$

Note: Non-operating items such as payment of interest, income from dividend, profit or loss from the sale of the investment, etc., are excluded in the operating profit calculation.

Net Profit Margin

Net profit is the final amount arrived at after adjusting all kinds of operating and non-operating items, and this entire profit amount belongs to the equity shareholders of the company.

As we've already discussed, a single figure in a company's report is not enough to analyse the overall performance. So, to draw a comparative study, we need to calculate Net Profit Margin, which shows the proportion of net income to total sales.

After looking at net profit margin, you can make out the proportion of revenues that goes towards settling operating and non-operating expenses, and the percentage that's left over for either distributing to shareholders or reinvesting in the company.

Performing similar calculations as before, we can see that net profit margin for HeadLabs is 39.37 per cent.

If you're thinking that this is quite impressive, here's the complete picture.

You see, net profit for HeadLabs includes other income of Rs 60 lakh, which is almost 75 per cent of the core revenue. There's no guarantee that HeadLabs will be able to generate this income in the future as well.

Investor Alert!

If you see a substantial amount of other income in the income statement of the company, then it's a caveat for you. You need to evaluate the nature of this other income critically and then take a decision.

This was all about profit margins. Now, we need to consider the scenario from an investor's point of view.

HeadLabs Goes Public

After completing a successful year of operations, in 2015, HeadLabs went public. The shares were issued to the public and got subscribed. This resulted in HeadLabs raising Rs 200 lakh (or Rs 2 crore) from the public, thereby increasing the share capital to Rs 300 lakh (or Rs 3 crore).

2016 turns out to be a fantastic year for HeadLabs.

P/L account of HeadLabs in 2016

	Amount (in Rs lakh)
Revenue from sales	140
Other income (commissions, dividends, etc.)	60
Total income	**200**
Less: Expenses	
Cost of raw materials	(65)
Rent	(10)
Administrative expenses	(30)
Depreciation (wear and tear)	(10)
Interest	(10)
Other expenses (non-operating)	(5)
Profit before tax	**70**
Less: Tax at 30%	21
Net profit	**49**

Balance sheet of HeadLabs in 2016

	Amount (in Rs lakh)
Share capital (Money given by Kumar's father + Money received from IPO)	300
Reserve and surplus	80.5
Long-term borrowing (business loan)	50
Short-term borrowing (Money borrowed from friends for short term)	30

	Amount (in Rs lakh)
Current liabilities	40.5
Total liabilities	**501**
Fixed assets	180
Capital work in progress	100
Investment	60
Cash	105
Inventory	20
Other current assets	36
Total assets	**501**

The second year of operations brought a great opportunity for HeadLabs. The company received a bulk order from an international business process outsourcing unit or BPO, which rewarded them with an increase of profit by more than 50 per cent over their last year's profit.

So, the total profit equalled Rs 49 lakh.

Impressive, right? But it's not about the company's gains. It's about what the shareholders got.

An investor puts his money in a company with the hope of a good return.

If a company generates huge profits and also requires a high amount of capital investment, then returns for the shareholders will not increase. So, the company will not be able to maximize its shareholders' wealth.

This is where we use Return on Equity (ROE). So, the bigger financial picture of HeadLabs will look like the following:

Net profit in 2015 = Rs 31.5 lakh (with a capital requirement of Rs 131.5 lakh)

Net profit in 2016 = Rs 49 lakh (with a capital requirement
of Rs 380.5)
So, return on equity (ROE) in 2015 = 23.95%
While ROE in 2016 = 12.88%

ROE is one of the most important ratios for potential investors
because it indicates how efficient the company is in generating
returns on the investment done by its shareholders.

A high ROE indicates a company's ability to generate
high returns for its shareholders. If a company reinvests
its earnings wisely and is able to enhance productivity
and profits, it can increase its ROE, thereby enhancing
shareholders' wealth.

Investors need to understand that profitability and income
levels vary significantly across sectors, so this yardstick (ROE)
cannot be used to compare inter-sector companies. Also, a
short-term slide in profit may lead to a low ROE.

So, evaluate the ROE for 3–5 years to spot companies
with a track record of stable profitability.

The major drawback of ROE is that it only shows returns
generated by equity investment. But equity is not the only way
by which a company can raise funds. It can also take a loan,
can't it?

If a company takes a huge amount of borrowed money
compared to equity capital, then the ROE percentage will be
high.

In capital-intensive industries such as iron and steel,
automobile, real estate, etc., companies rely more on debt than
equity. So, ROE will not present the right picture in the case
of these companies. Instead, Return on Capital Employed or
ROCE will provide a more reliable picture.

$$\text{ROCE} = \frac{\text{Earnings before interest and tax EBIT x 100}}{\text{Share capital } + \text{ Reserve and surplus } + \text{ Borrowings}}$$

Using this formula, we see that for HeadLabs,

$$\text{ROCE} = \frac{80\text{x}100}{460.5} = 17.37\%$$

It should be noted that, while calculating ROCE, we use earnings before interest and taxes (EBIT) and not profits before taxes (PBT) as it is the return generated by the company on the capital 'employed' by it, which includes both equity and debt.

A company's ROCE should always be greater than its cost of capital; otherwise, it's likely to go bankrupt in the near future. Imagine if a company pays an annual interest of Rs 50 crore on a loan of Rs 500 crore, the cost of capital will be 10 per cent. Now, if the ROCE is less than 10 per cent, the company is not able to employ its capital efficiently. And if this situation continues, the company might face survival issues in the future.

But sometimes, ROE is also not an effective measure.

Suppose you spot another company in the same industry called Bass-X, whose ROCE is 14 per cent with a similar capital structure but almost negligible cash. Do you think that's a better option?

Of course not!

The balance sheet of HeadLabs includes a cash balance of Rs 105 lakh, which is not employed in business operations. Had the cash been used, HeadLabs would probably have had a higher ROCE.

Cash is an idle asset. So, to eliminate the effect caused by the cash factor, Return on Invested Capital or ROIC is used.

$$ROIC = \frac{\text{Earnings before interest and tax (EBIT) x 100}}{\text{Share capital + Reserve and surplus + Borrowings − cash in hand}}$$

$$\text{ROIC of HeadLabs} = \frac{80 \times 100}{355.5} = 22.50\%$$

ROIC of Bass-X = 14% (since cash balance for Bass-X = 0)

Usually, a company with a higher ROIC is better for an investor. But, since there is unused cash, it is something to analyse critically.

Investor Alert!

For a company, if the cash balance has been high for the last 4–5 years and it is not being utilized, that's not a good sign. Had the company been planning an acquisition, it's understandable, but idle cash kept for years with no use creates dissatisfaction among investors.

Activity or Efficiency Ratios

Profitability ratios present a clear picture of how much profit a company is making in a particular period of time. But will the profitability sustain? This is equally important, and this is presented by efficiency ratios, also known as activity ratios.

In simple terms, efficiency is the ability to enhance the output with a given input. Similarly, efficiency ratios also tell us whether a company will be able to enhance its profit if it has more assets at its disposal.

The following are all efficiency ratios.

Account Payable Turnover/Creditors Turnover Ratio

The Account Payable Turnover Ratio is used to see how efficiently a company pays its suppliers and short-term debts.

Accounts payable is a short-term debt that a company owes to its suppliers, vendors, or other creditors. The payable turnover ratio can also be referred to in terms of time period, known as 'creditor days.' It shows the average time (in days) that a company takes to pay its suppliers.

Generally, a longer period of credit (high creditor days) is considered an advantage because it represents a source of free finance for the company.

Large corporations generally have better negotiating power with suppliers, and that is why they enjoy favourable credit terms, which helps them maintain a high credit period.

Asset Turnover Ratio

Asset Turnover Ratio is used to determine how efficiently a company utilizes its assets to generate sales. The ratio compares sales with average assets.

Generally, a low asset turnover ratio suggests idle capacity, poor receivables management, bad acquisition, or economic slowdown.

Companies with cyclical business models tend to have volatile asset turnover ratios. So, the ratio should be evaluated for several time periods. Companies with low profit margins usually have high asset turnover, signifying efficiency in managing resources, which thereby helps them to provide a high ROE despite having a low profit margin. For example, retail giants like Big Bazaar, DMart, etc., operate on quite thin profit margins, but their asset turnover is very high due to the volumes they sell and their frequency of selling. That is why they are able to maintain a decent ROE.

Inventory Turnover Ratio

Improper inventory management can directly affect a company's profitability. Inventory management is mainly about cost and risk. Transportation charges, storage, opportunity cost, and insurance cost, are examples of cost. Likewise, obsolescence, shelf-life, understocking, wear and tear, pilferage, etc. are examples of risk.

Inventory turnover ratio is the proportion of cost of goods sold to average inventory. Investors should examine the Inventory Turnover Ratio in order to determine the number of times a company has sold and replaced its inventory in a year. A low inventory turnover ratio indicates poor liquidity, overstocking, and risk of obsolescence. However, this has to be checked, keeping the industry benchmarks in mind.

Debtor/Receivable Turnover Ratio

There are very few businesses that operate fully on a no-credit policy. Although a favourable credit policy offers a competitive advantage to the company, it also bears the additional risk of bad debts. So, prompt collection from debtors is an essential step for maintaining healthy cash flows.

A high turnover ratio can be interpreted as the management's conservative credit policy and effective collection method.

Investor Alert!

Debtor turnover and inventory turnover ratios are also vital tools to check for accounting scandals. Many times, companies inflate their sales volume either through channel stuffing or through fictitious sales. So, any unusual increase in receivables or inventory should be evaluated with sales trends. If it has a negative correlation or if there is a huge difference in proportionate changes, it can be an indication of fraudulent financial reporting.

Solvency Ratios

Debt can be the death of any company. The Indian market has seen plenty of examples like Jet Airways, Kingfisher, Reliance Communications, etc. These companies used to be everyone's favourites in the stock market at one point in time. But now, we all know where they are.

The likelihood of a company going bankrupt is evident from solvency ratios.

There are two components of solvency ratios:

1. Debt–equity ratio
2. Interest coverage ratio

The proportion of the amount raised by a company through debt and that raised through equity is shown by the debt–

equity ratio. A figure of less than one is always preferred. This is because a higher ratio indicates a higher proportion of debt in the company's capital structure.

Investor Alert!

Debt is a fixed obligation. Defaulting invites great trouble. Therefore, investors must be careful if a company's debt–equity ratio is quite high.

Here's a fun fact: Debt is a cheaper source to raise funds as compared to equity. The reason is that tax benefit can be claimed with interest paid on debt, while it cannot be claimed in case of paying dividends.

Debt is usually projected as a monster, but it is not so. Depending on the financial position of the company, the debt can be beneficial as well. Consider a company in excellent financial health. If it has a project on hand and doesn't want to dilute its shareholders' wealth, it can raise the money through debt.

What's the optimum level of debt a company can have? This is calculated with the help of interest coverage ratio, which measures the ease with which a company can pay its interest liability on the outstanding debt. It is expressed as:

$$\text{Interest Coverage Ratio} = \frac{\text{Earnings before interest and taxes}}{\text{Interest expense}}$$

The higher the interest coverage ratio, the better it is for the investor.

Liquidity Ratios

Too much long-term thinking is sometimes harmful because we're living in the present and being too futuristic can take us far away from reality. For a company, simply maintaining solvency isn't enough. It has to take care of liquidity as well.

For instance, owning land worth Rs 1 crore won't help the company pay off an electricity bill of, say, Rs 10,000. Thus, it becomes important for a company to possess assets like cash, marketable securities, etc. (called current assets) to be able to pay all its dues on time.

In terms of investing, several liquidity ratios are used to ascertain a company's liquidity. These ratios measure the ease with which a company can pay its dues.

Furthermore, these ratios should be compared with the industry average or historical data, as companies with different business models have to maintain different levels of working capital.

One liquidity ratio is the current ratio, defined as the proportion of current assets to current liabilities.

Let's take a look at the current ratio for HeadLabs.

$$\text{Current Ratio} = \frac{161}{40.5} = 3.97 \text{ times}$$

Ideally, the current ratio should be in the range of 1 to 2. A high current ratio shows that the company has enough current assets to pay off its current liabilities on time. But a very high figure shows that the current assets of the company are lying idle.

There's a slight limitation to the current ratio. There are certain current assets that can't be readily liquidated, such as inventory and prepaid expenses. So, to accurately judge the immediate liquidity of the company, we use quick ratio.

Quick ratio is the ease with which the company can pay its short-term obligations without liquidating its fixed assets.

$$\text{Quick Ratio of HeadLabs} = \frac{141}{40.5} = 3.48$$

Investor Alert!

The gap between the current ratio and quick ratio of the company, indicates the amount of money that is blocked in inventory. The investor should compare the company's data with its competitors to ensure how efficiently the company is managing its inventory. Also, the investor should analyse the trend for the last few years.

Moral of the Story

The ratios discussed in the story are not predefined criteria for analysing a stock perfectly because each ratio's usage is subjective depending upon the company, industry, etc. As an investor, your criteria will differ based on the companies you analyse, just like a customer who doesn't apply a single criterion to purchase anything and everything.

19

Valuation Analysis

A company's market price does not always denote its 'fair value' because the stock price is determined by market forces (demand and supply). There are numerous external factors that may temporarily affect stock prices (like a favourable government regulation), but the sudden optimism or pessimism is short-lived and that is why fair value is considered. In the long run, stock prices tend to align with the company's fundamentals and reach what we call fair value.

There are various methods to arrive at the fair value of a company. The method you choose will depend upon the industry and the business model of the company. Below are some really important methods for your reference.

Discounting Cash Flows

As the name signifies, the method estimates the profitability of an investment by calculating its future income or cash flow and then discounting this income with a reasonable rate of return called the discount rate. The valuation analysis focuses on determining the value of the company today, based on future cash-flow projection.

To understand it better, we will take an example of real estate investment.

Suppose you are interested in buying a house to earn rental income from it. What price will you be willing to pay?

First of all, let's see the benefits you will get from this:

- Monthly rental income
- Capital gain after selling the house

Let's assume you want to hold the house for five years.

In these five years, suppose you expect to collect a total rent of Rs 3 lakh (at Rs 5,000 per month) and plan to sell off the house for Rs 20 lakh after five years.

So, in this case, you will not pay more than the total rent you will earn in these five years plus the expected selling price after five years. Similarly, paying an amount equal to the sum of rental income and sale realization will not make sense, because you will not gain anything if your total revenue is equal to your total expense. So, the fair value for this investment is less than Rs 23 lakh. The lesser, the better!

The key to understanding this is that your purchase price should undoubtedly be less than your total expected income, i.e., your future cash flows. Additionally, only considering future cash flows won't help you to arrive at a fair value. As we know, one rupee will not be worth as much in the future as it is today, going by the general concept of inflation. So, here we need to adjust the figure to make it directly comparable to the present value. It is the basic idea behind Discounted Cash Flow (DCF) Analysis.

Let's see how this figure is calculated.

Present value

$$= \frac{CF_1}{(1+r)^1} + \frac{CF_2}{(1+r)^2} + \frac{CF_3}{(1+r)^3} + \cdots + \frac{CF_n}{(1+r)^n}$$
$$+ \text{ Terminal value} - \text{Debt}$$

Where CF is the amount of cash flow in a year. CF_1 is for the first year, CF_2 is for the second year, and so on.

r is the discount rate or expected rate of return, and

n is the number of years for which future cash flow occurs.

To simplify this, let's take an example. Your friend offers you a deal where you will get Rs 6,000 every year for the next five years. And for this, you need to pay Rs 25,000 today. Will you accept this deal?

If you simply see the cash flows, the total future income would be Rs 30,000 (Rs 6,000 × 5). And you need to pay Rs 25,000 upfront. So, your gain will be Rs 5,000.

But is it really worth it?

Assuming an interest rate of 8 per cent per annum, an investment of Rs 25,000 in a fixed deposit scheme will give you Rs 36,700. So why not invest in a fixed deposit which also comes with almost *zero* risk?

Then how much would you offer for this deal? The amount depends on your target rate of return. Let's say you expect a return of 12 per cent per annum for undertaking an additional risk instead of putting the amount in an FD. So, in this case, the present value or DCF will be Rs 21,628.

Hence, a purchase value below Rs 21,628 would be called a good buy, and this exact amount would be the fair value.

Similarly, when you invest in any shares or buy a whole business, you need to figure out the right price by analysing the expected cash flows. The important thing to note here is DCF analysis won't be applicable for all firms. Companies with relatively stable cash flows in industries like FMCG, pharma, and utilities are most suitable for DCF analysis. Real estate, steel, automobiles, or other industries that are exposed to a significant degree of cyclicality cannot be valued through this method.

Sum of the Parts Valuation (SOTP)

This method determines the net value of a firm by separately examining the value of each investment done by the company through different business units, associates, or subsidiaries.

Let's understand this with an interesting example:

How do you think McDonald's decides the price of a combo? It's quite obvious that they add the individual costs of the components and then decide the final price. Also, the price of the combo would cost somewhere around the sum of the actual individual prices.

Similarly, there are many large corporations that are engaged in diversified sets of business activities across different industries.

Since the nature of revenue and cash flows of different companies vary depending upon the type of industry in which they operate, the valuation of a conglomerate or a holding company cannot be calculated with one method. So, for this, we need to calculate the value of each business unit. The aggregate value of these units will be the intrinsic value or the fair value of the holding unit.

Let us see the valuation of a holding company, say Bajaj Holdings and Investments Ltd, considering its investments.

Bajaj Holdings and Investments had a market capitalization of Rs 36,192 crore (as of 2019). It held shares in the companies listed in the following table.

Companies in which Bajaj Holdings and Investments held shares (all given figures are in Rs crore)

S. No.	Name of the company	Proportion of holding	Market cap of the company	Bajaj Holdings and Investments' share
1.	Bajaj Auto Ltd	33.43%	80,648	26,960.62
2.	Bajaj Finserv Ltd	39.29%	1,13,298	44,514.78
3.	Bajaj Auto Holdings Ltd	100%		25
4.	Maharashtra Scooters	51%	4,373	2,230.23
Total value of investments of Bajaj Holdings and Investments				73,730.63

Although the market capitalization of Bajaj Holdings and Investments Ltd is Rs 36,192 crore, the investments held by this company total Rs 73,730.63 crore. Holding companies are generally valued at around 20–30 per cent less than the value of their investments, owing to complications involved in transferring profits.

In 2019, Bajaj Holdings and Investments was trading at a discount of almost 50 per cent of total value of its holdings, reflecting its undervaluation by the market.

Relative Valuation Method

The methods described till now are absolute measures to calculate the intrinsic value without reference to any peer entity, industry average, or market benchmark. However, there are several types of companies for which investors need to rely more on market behaviour, i.e., the way the market values companies in different economic situations and market levels.

The basic idea behind this method is to identify similar types of companies and conduct a comparative analysis to calculate the value of the firm.

The following are types of relative valuation metrics with the industries in which they're used:

- Price to Earnings ratio (P/E): FMCG, IT, pharma
- Price to Book value ratio (P/B): Banking, Non-Banking Financial Companies (NBFCs), real estate
- Price to Sales ratio (P/S): Automobile, textile
- Enterprise value to operating profit ratio (EV/EBITDA): Airline, telecom, automobile
- Price to Free Cash Flow to the Firm ratio (P/FCFF): Oil and gas, steel

Let us discuss these, one by one.

P/E Ratio

This is the most widely used tool to compare the valuation of different stocks. The ratio gives you an idea of the amount you're paying for each rupee of a company's earnings.

$$P/E \text{ ratio } = \frac{\text{Price}}{\text{EPS}}$$

Where Price = Current market price of a share
EPS = Earnings per share (Net profit / Number of shares)

For example, if the market price of the share is Rs 20 and EPS is Rs 5, then the

P/E ratio of the company = 20/5 = 4

This signifies that an investor is willing to pay Rs 20 to buy a share that is currently generating an EPS of Rs 5 per year, i.e., the investor is willing to pay four times the amount actually earned by each unit of the company in the year.

Why are investors paying four times for the share?

A higher P/E ratio usually expresses how expensive a stock is being traded in the market. Investors' expectations in the long term and their speculation of brand value prompt them to pay a higher amount. This is because they have to buy the share once, and they expect the company to keep generating earnings every year so that their earnings in the long term will be far in excess of the price they pay to buy the share.

Should you always buy stocks with lower P/E ratios?

Novice investors can often make the mistake of buying stocks based only on the P/E ratio since the ratio can be misleading sometimes.

As we know, higher the net profit of the company, higher will be its EPS and thus, lower the P/E ratio.

A higher net profit can be due to two possible reasons:

- A higher operating profit due to better performance of the company.
- Some extraordinary profits earned by the company during the year.

A higher net profit due to increased efficiency and turnover of the company are beneficial for the shareholders, but if it is due to extraordinary transactions such as the sale of property or any windfall gains, then we need to be cautious.

So, an investor should always dig deeper and find the reasons for the low P/E ratio because if it is on account of extraordinary profits, it is temporary. Investment in such companies will not necessarily benefit the shareholders.

How do you decide that the P/E ratio is not very high?

For this, we have to consider the Price/Earnings to growth (PEG) ratio. The PEG ratio is based on the premise that a company should have an earnings growth rate that can justify its P/E ratio.

Ideally, this PEG ratio should be less than or equal to 1, i.e., growth > P/E.

In the example above, suppose the EPS growth rate is 2 per cent, then,

PEG ratio will be 4/2 = 2

Therefore, this company is probably overpriced.

P/B Ratio

Earnings are not the proper measure for evaluating companies with a huge asset base, like banks, NBFCs, real estate companies, etc. Since profit tends to fluctuate depending upon the economic condition, government policy, and other macroeconomic factors, the more appropriate parameter is the ratio of price to book value per share.

The P/B ratio measures the market value of the firm in relation to its book value per share, where book value per share of a company is the value of assets proportional to each share of the company.

Let's say a company, which is trading at a price of Rs 150, has a total asset base of Rs 1,00,000, and its liabilities amount to Rs 20,000.

In this case, the funds belonging to the shareholders, or the net worth of the company = Rs 1,00,000 - 20,000 = Rs 80,000.

So, if the number of shares is 1,000, the book value per share is Rs 80 (Rs 80,000/1,000), and

P/B ratio = 150/80 = 1.86

Ideally, a P/B ratio of 1 is considered to be fairly valued, and a ratio of less than 1 indicates undervalued stock.

However, like the P/E ratio, the P/B ratio can also be distorted. Any kind of acquisitions, asset impairment, or share buybacks can affect the ratio significantly. Furthermore, the ratio also ignores off-balance-sheet items, such as contingent liabilities, and thus deflates the total liabilities. In the case of banking companies also, a low P/B ratio does not necessarily indicate undervaluation; it may be due to worsening asset quality, i.e., high non-performing asset (NPA).

So, investors should look at the P/B ratio vis-à-vis ROE, as it gives an idea about the efficiency with which capital is employed in addition to the relative valuation.

P/S Ratio

The price to sales ratio values the company based on its turnover and not on profits. This method of valuation effectively assesses companies that possess a high growth potential but are currently unable to make profits. There are certain industries that are exposed to a high degree of cyclicality and have a long gestation period, like the automobile industry. During the initial stage of the business, profitability is not an appropriate way to measure the performance of the company. In these industries, the P/S ratio works as an effective tool to determine the valuation of the company.

EV/EBITDA

Enterprise value (EV) is the theoretical 'takeover price' of a company.

The ownership of a company is rooted in its shares. So, if you want to buy a company, i.e., gain 100 per cent control over its management, you need to buy all the shares from the market.

So, your cash outflow for buying the control of the company = Market price per share × Number of shares (i.e., the market cap of the company)

But when you get complete ownership of the company, all the assets and the liabilities of the company belong to you. Now, consider this. You paid the price of market capital, which is determined by market forces, to buy actual assets and liabilities. In contrast, the actual cost of acquisition will be the sum of all the privileges (to use the assets) and obligations (to pay back the loans) you get once you buy the business.

Enterprise value finds the actual cost of acquisition of the business. It is calculated as follows:

Enterprise value = Market capitalization + Debt – (Cash + Bank balance)

As soon as you buy the business, the cash belonging to the company now belongs to you (the owner), and the debt liability is also your responsibility now. Thus, cash is reduced from the cost, while debt is added.

To make a comparative valuation analysis of two similar companies:

Investors can use the EV/EBITDA ratio to calculate the entire value of the business. The major significance of EV/EBITDA is that it removes the effect of non-cash items such as depreciation and amortization (EBITDA stands for earnings before interest, taxes, depreciation, and amortization) and considers the real earnings of the company.

The higher the enterprise value (greater numerator), the higher will be the ratio, indicating that the business is expensive.

P/FCFF Ratio

Free Cash Flow to the Firm (FCFF) basically means the amount of cash flow generated by the firm in a particular period of time after adjusting for all its operational and capital expenditures. Since this cash flow is determined after adjusting all expenditures, it can be effectively used by a company to generate additional revenues. Therefore, a firm with more FCFF has better chances of expansion.

The Price to FCFF ratio is used to carry out a comparative study of free cash flow and market cap of the company. If P/FCFF is 5, it means that for every rupee of free cash flow generated, the market is paying Rs 5. In general, the lower, the better.

Earnings and revenue can be easily manipulated, but not cash flow. Therefore, this ratio gives a more accurate picture for valuation.

How to Use These Methods

The methods of valuation we've just discussed are very important to know, but actually using them is more important. As we've already discussed, investing is not a science; it's an art, and therefore, it's not based on a sure-shot formula. Please note that these methods cannot be used as is because the performance of companies and industries cannot be predicted accurately. It is advised that investors always use their discretion while investing.

20

Behavioural Biases

The Illusion Creators

As you've read earlier, behavioural biases affect our routine decisions, including those related to investing in stock, to a significant extent. So, it is important to identify such biases and remove them to make the best investment decisions possible. Let's look at a few biases.

Familiarity Bias towards Known Brands/Names

Familiarity bias is the most common bias seen in everyday life. Under this bias, investors tend to overweigh the stocks of the companies they work for, or they may be biased towards the stocks of brand names they are aware of.

An example is choosing Britannia biscuits over Sunfeast because you are more familiar with the Britannia brand. Likewise, you might end up picking up Britannia's stock over ITC.

Some other day-to-day examples are following the same route to work or home, visiting the same store, again and again for shopping for daily needs, wearing the clothes of particular brands, eating the same the flavour of ice cream every time, etc.

Although the theory of investment insists that investors must thoroughly research and analyse stocks before picking, stock investors usually invest in public sector securities influenced by their familiarity and comfort.

When individuals invest in the same company they are working for, they don't realize that they are doubly risking their money. In case the company does not perform well, then the employee may suffer a reduced salary income as well as reduced returns on the investments. Hence, investing in the company you work for may require you to do a thorough analysis, such as considering the tax benefits, calculating the anticipated returns, analysing the industry performance, transaction costs, etc. But the familiarity bias drives investors so firmly that they blindly invest in the companies they have been working in for a few years.

This bias is commonly seen in individuals who love to live within their comfort zones. Such individuals fear to travel the untrodden path as unfamiliarity makes them uneasy.

Representativeness

Representativeness is a widespread bias that is governed by the image, representation, or past performance of a company. For instance, if an investor considers a company to be a good company, then he may instantly choose to invest in it. But this can be misleading, as a company's brand image cannot judge its exact worth. Conventionally, the image of a company is enhanced due to advertisements and promotional activities.

There are two types of representative biases:

a. *Horizontal Bias:* This bias says that people tend to value a stock based on the track record of its peers. So, they try to forecast the performance of the stock in the future based on the similarities with its analogues.

b. *Vertical Bias:* Investors often take the past performance of stocks as representative of their future performance. Investors tend to make decisions on the basis of past facts and not the present or future prospects. Such biases are also often referred to as recency biases. The chasing of recent trends is a part of technical analysis and not value investing.

For example, Cadbury was known to manufacture delicious, good-quality chocolates until there were a couple of incidents where worms were reportedly found in its chocolates. This reporting immediately tarnished the brand image of Cadbury, which brought down the value of its stocks.

Do these biases help in making the right investments?

The answer is both yes and no, as it depends on the term of investment you have chosen. For small-term investments, the past performance at times develops a negative correlation with near-future performance. But for long-term investments, the past performance tends to establish a positive relationship with future performance.

Interestingly, the availability of information enhances representative bias. When the availability of specific information like extended news coverage of high-performing stocks spreads like wildfire, it grabs the attention of potential investors immediately. Such news stimulates the trading of shares due to the development of immediate biases towards them.

Anchoring

Anchoring refers to using irrelevant information as a basis to make financial investments. It may also be put as getting fixated on past information and using it to make inappropriate financial investments.

For example, an investor may get far too influenced by the buying cost of security. And he may use it as a reference to evaluate investing in that particular financial stock. In the context of spending, market participants with this bias exist prominently everywhere.

Anchoring bias is commonly seen in both naïve and professional investors. However, the latter have more access

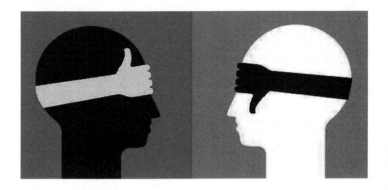

and exposure to investments to gauge if they are letting these biases influence them.

For example, suppose you want to buy a property, and you get an initial quote of Rs 10 lakh for a flat. This works as a reference point for you. After a few months pass, the market crashes, and the prices of the property fall. Now, if your dealer quotes you Rs 9 lakh for the same property, you might like it without being aware that the current price is Rs 8 lakh. This happens because you got anchored to the initial price quote of Rs 10 lakh, and so anything lesser than that would mean a good deal to you.

The same principle works in stock investment too. You have seen security priced at Rs 100, and you want to purchase it but find it overpriced. So you wait for the price to plunge, and the moment it touches Rs 80, you jump up and grab the stock. But had you not been anchored to the initial hiked price of Rs 100, you would have waited further to see if the price fell further. Later, you got to know that the price dropped to Rs 65 just a week later. Now, do you think that holding on to the initial pricing was wise?

Beginner's Luck in Investing

All of us often experience beginner's luck in one or many instances. Remember winning the first time you played Business, Scrabble, or Ludo games? On winning the game the very first time we played, we would get so excited, and we always thought that we had mastered the game right on the first go.

But what happened when you played the game a few more times? Did you continue achieving the same success, or did you lose many games? Well, the first time you won was due to beginner's luck, which is when a beginner experiences unexpected success against a seasoned or professional player in a chosen activity.

The Reason behind Beginner's Luck

Beginner's luck leads to success on the first go because a beginner is free of anchoring bias, which refers to anchoring or holding on to a piece of information usually related to the past.

For example, if a seasoned investor had seen shares of MRF tyre trading at Rs 100, and now the same company is trading at Rs 1,000, then he will be reluctant to buy the shares for Rs 1,000 because it was available to him for Rs 100 some time ago. But if a naïve investor with no investment background looks at the share price of MRF tyre, then he will take Rs 1,000 as the base value and happily choose to invest in it if it seems promising.

Hence, beginner's luck was due to a lack of price anchoring in this case and not due to real luck.

Overconfidence Bias

Overconfidence refers to an investor having a bias towards his prediction skills, his judgements about the market behaviour, and his cognitive abilities.

In these biases, the investor tends to overestimate not just his prediction skills but also the information that he receives. In simple words, the investor is overenthusiastic and may act immediately based on an investment tip that he gets from an advisor or that he reads somewhere.

The investor with this bias considers himself smarter than other investors and advisors. This brings in a lot of overconfidence, and he starts acting as per his perceived knowledge of investment.

The following are some examples of overconfidence bias.

- *Over-ranking:* In this case, an overconfident investor ranks his knowledge and performance higher than that of others.
- *Timing:* Usually, an investor may invest in a specific period, assuming the company will start performing

outstandingly, rendering good profits on investment. In reality, business projects are always underestimated for timings and are mostly delayed beyond the proposed schedules.

- *Desirability effect:* Sometimes, investors get desperate to get the desired results. In such situations, the investor will overestimate the possibility of something happening, but the probability of such happenings, in reality, is very low.

The types of overconfidence bias are as follows:

a. *Prediction Bias:* Prediction biases usually occur while making frequent investments. Investments based on predictions can be far removed from reality. Let's say I am an overconfident investor predicting a 7–8 per cent gain or fall in stock, and I invest based on this prediction. But the real fluctuation in prices turn out to be 15 per cent, which is revealed later. I fell into the trap of prediction bias.

The negative aspect of this type of bias is that you may underestimate the risk involved in investing in a stock.

b. *Certainty Bias:* This bias refers to being overconfident about considering a particular investment to be a good one. This leads to the investor trading too often or too much at a time. Also, these kinds of investors end up building highly concentrated portfolios without doing thorough research on the stocks they invest in, inviting much higher risks of incurring losses in the future.

Now, let us see the implications of overconfidence in detail.

Excessive Trading

Overconfidence often results in excessive trading. Since the investors are overconfident about their knowledge, this makes them trade more often. As per M. Zuckerman, due to the overconfidence bias, an investor turns into a sensation-seeking personality with the following features:

- *Deriving thrill:* The adventure-seeking desire engages the person to keep trying their hand at trading.
- *The desire to gain experience:* The investor desires to gain hands-on experience by working on something new and exciting.
- *No inhibition:* Trading is an accepted activity that is appropriate as per social norms. So, when an investor trades often, he is gambling to mint money, which is within the legal framework. Thus, an overconfident investor gets deeper into trading and does it even more.
- *Fun and excitement:* Trading shares is fun for some investors and kills boredom.
- *Excessively optimistic:* Overconfident investors are overly optimistic about the companies they are tracking. Their assumptions are miscalculated and are overrated as compared to reality.

Under-Diversification

As we saw, with the certainty bias, overconfident investors tend to opt for a concentrated portfolio because they are super confident about their investments and put in all their money in a few chosen stocks. This results in under-diversification. While this is also a trait of seasoned investors, the approach they take is very different compared to overconfident investors.

Seasoned investors thoroughly analyse the funds, the companies, the markets, and the industries and take a patient and calculated approach to generate a concentrated portfolio that will give promising returns in the future. But overconfident investors tend to invest money without doing any thorough research. These investors believe themselves to be smart enough to make the right decisions and end up generating an under-diversified portfolio.

Herd Mentality Bias

Man is a social being. He does not like to be cut out from a trend or opt-out from a movement, and marketers know this very well. They try to position a product to create a brand in a way that people start relating to it. So the brand becomes a trend, and others blindly follow it to be part of a social norm.

In this bias, an investor tends to copy other investors. This type of bias is dominated by an investor's instinct and emotions rather than the analytical approach taken to understand a stock before investing in it.

The herd mentality is thoroughly hard-wired in us, and we often act unconsciously as per this mentality. It is due to the following two reasons:

a. *Social pressure:* Man as a social being seeks acceptance and approval of others. This is why he follows a trend or norm.
b. *The belief that a large group of people cannot be wrong:* A man tends to copy others because he thinks that so many people who have chosen to follow the same path cannot be wrong.

Now let us consider a few real-world examples.

Example 1

Suppose you visit Noida for the first time, and you are looking for a good restaurant to dine at. Suddenly, you come across two posh-looking restaurants opposite to each other on a street. Now, because you are new, you don't have any clue as to which of the two is good. As you approach the restaurants, you see that one is filled with plenty of youngsters and the other is empty. So you think that the crowded one must be the one serving good food, and you choose to eat there. Afterwards, you felt that the food quality was average and the food was just palatable.

Later, you dig deeper and go around the locality, asking about those two restaurants. To your great surprise, you discover that the one filled with youngsters was visited by college students on a sponsored outing because it gave massive discounts on group outings. And the restaurant opposite to it is consistently better in terms of food quality and taste. But it had just opened at the time when you visited the place, so you saw it empty.

So you see how the herd mentality bias made you take a decision that acted against your interest?

Example 2

Another example is that in a democratic country like India, politicians are chosen to a great extent by herd mentality bias. Such biases are strongly visible in people from the middle and lower classes of society who tend to follow each other. The result of such a majority has not always been favourable in the past. The democratically chosen politicians were not the best of the lot at all times.

The same dynamics work in stock investment as well. What the majority of people choose may not be the right option.

Example 3

A famous example of a herd mentality bias in financial investment is investing in smartphone manufacturing companies.

When Blackberry was launched, it became the talk of the town. All top officials shifted to Blackberry, making it an expensive buy that was sought after by all youngsters. Many technology companies like Blackberry do successfully make a lot of noise in the market but often lack a good business model.

But because Blackberry became a big sensation at one point in time, most investors started investing in it. And naïve or biased investors followed the crowd and invested in it. But the reality was very different, and eventually, Blackberry was thrown out of the market by other strong smartphone players like Apple, Sony, etc.

The herd mentality bias is so strong that if an investor is advised to act contrarily to what the majority of people are doing, then it may even instil fear. Not many investors have the guts to invest based on functional analysis and research because that may mean acting contrarily to other investors. No wonder. Avoiding herd mentality is considered to be the golden rule of investment! Investors do get carried away by the mass behaviour of other investors, and that is quite natural. This is why behavioural finance needs to be learnt to enhance financial decision-making skills.

So how do you keep yourself from falling prey to the herd mentality syndrome?

This is one of the most common questions asked by new investors! You need to dig deeper into analysing the prospects of the investment before investing in it. The more you know about a company's stock, the better your chances are of not falling into the herd mentality bias trap.

Commitment Bias

People with commitment bias develop an attachment to their past ideas and beliefs, so much so that they invariably keep applying those ideas to new situations. Commitment bias is also referred to as self-serving bias.

Commitment bias is usually seen in our day-to-day lives when we do things or take decisions only to approve or justify our past actions. It is like a slippery slope where a single slip is enough to pull you down completely.

For example, you seek help from a group of friends, but only one friend chooses to help you. Now, the next time you approach the same group for help, you are more likely to receive it from the same friend who helped you earlier. This is because that compassionate friend will choose to stay consistent with his effort in the past. He seems to be a value-driven person who would like to stick to the commitments he has made for himself. This is a typical example of commitment bias. An investor can hold on to a security longer than he had thought of holding just because he chose to invest in it, even when it is contrary to his interest.

Commitment bias, in simple words, is like having a belief that the decisions we took in the past were good. It is the belief that tells us to refrain from disinvesting quickly, even when holding on to some stocks may result in a big loss.

This is why some legendary investors never openly suggest names of good stocks to invest in on any public platform like news channels, newspapers, etc. If a seasoned investor suggests buying a stock on a public platform, and later he finds some flaws with this stock, do you think he will be able to change his suggestion? Definitely not! Because now the advisor is a victim of commitment bias.

Hence, it is essential to do your own research in stock investment, as you do not know whether the advisor is suffering from commitment bias.

Confirmation Bias

Confirmation bias indicates the tendency to use a piece of information to support your perceived notions and ignore information contrary to your beliefs.

For example, if an investor is interested in investing in Airtel, then he will look for positive information that supports his decision. Hence, if such an investor comes across any negative piece of information about the company, he may tend to overlook it.

A sound investment strategy is to always look for information that contradicts your way of thinking. This is what most successful investors have been doing. The point to note is that you need to approach investments with an open mind, as the shreds of evidence collected tend to flow in all different directions. Consequently, you will be able to analyse multiple perspectives, which will overcome any influences or biases present.

Confirmation bias occurs in two different circumstances as follows:

a. *Selective absorption of information:* When an investor selectively absorbs information from past situations and acts based on this particular information.

For example, you went to a hill station for a holiday and used a face compact with a good moisture-retaining capacity that made you look lovely. When you are back home, you experience hot tropical weather, and you think of using the same compact because you remember it gave you amazing results. But the performance of that compact is relative to the weather, so the hot weather makes your skin oily and sticky!

The reason behind this is that you selectively retained information about a make-up product. Of course, the same occurs in stock investment as well, where you need to consider many factors to check the performance of a stock.

b. *Misinterpretation of the information:* Confirmation bias is commonly seen when you misinterpret the information given to you.

Suppose you read somewhere that company X is bound to perform 100 times better in the coming decade if industrial norms are modified in that sector. But to make this happen, the government will have to alter its current taxation policies and structure.

So, as an investor, you keep track of this sector's developments. Suppose a few days later, you read that the government has chosen to modify two of its taxation policies to support the low and mid-cap companies in that sector.

But you misinterpret the information and think that the new change is for big companies like X. And based on this information, you invest in the company. After five years, you realize that the stock prices of company X have only marginally increased, which forces you to disinvest.

Here's another example of confirmation bias.

An investor came across a company Z, which is highly recommended by his colleague. With a lot of interest, the investor starts searching for supporting information to invest in that particular stock. Suppose he finds some supporting information, like a low debt-equity ratio or high cash inflow of the company, and some other danger signals like unfavourable policies. But he still chooses to invest in company Z under the influence of confirmation bias, only to be disappointed later.

Hindsight Bias

Hindsight bias is a term in psychology, which refers to the tendency of people to overestimate their ability to predict an outcome that could not have been practically possible to predict.

In investing, hindsight bias is pretty common. The pressure of investing in the right stock at the right time often ends up with investors frustrated at themselves for not knowing better or for not noticing the rising trends earlier.

People look for simpler solutions to complicated problems and thus tend to overthink and develop such biases. It is not that having these biases is wrong, but sometimes they can force the investor to find a wrong link between the cause and effect of investment.

Let's take the example of a trader who invests in the stock market. He has two options, either trading long or trading short. Trading long is buying a stock hoping that the stock price will rise. Trading short is borrowing a stock, selling it instantly with the idea of buying it back when the stock price decreases, and earning a considerable profit. The investor takes a long position, and unfortunately, the market responded contrary to his trade. He angrily claims that he knew this was going to happen, and that is hindsight bias.

Gambler's Fallacy

Gambler's fallacy is also called the Monte Carlo fallacy, or the fallacy of the Maturity of Chances. It is a widespread belief that if some event has occurred a few times in a given period, then it will happen less frequently in the future and vice-versa.

Gambler's fallacy is not correct, as the past event cannot govern the probability of occurrence of any game in the future.

So how does the gambler's fallacy work in financial investments?

Gambler's fallacy misleads investors who end up making the wrong decisions. Long-invested investors who witnessed constant growth in stock value over time liquidate their shares due to gambler's fallacy. This is because they believe that the value is more likely to decline after many consecutive gains.

Let's take the example of flipping a coin.

Suppose you are playing the game with your friend. The first five flips led to heads each time, but just before the sixth flip, you turn pessimist towards heads, and you feel that the sixth flip is more likely to be tails because the five earlier ones were heads.

But when you flip the coin, you see that the sixth flip is heads again! Why?

This is because the probability of getting heads or tails in each flip is 50 per cent, and each coin flip is completely independent of any past flips. It is a wholly independent event with a probability of 50 per cent each time. This is where a gambler's fallacy dilutes your conviction and makes you liquidate your asset only to prevent a loss that was, anyway not happening.

Disposition Effect

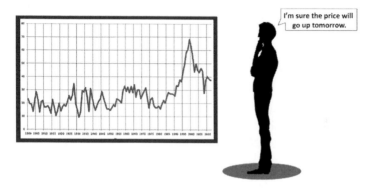

The disposition effect suggests that investors have an innate tendency to identify gains more quickly than to determine losses in any investment.

Selling security at a loss would mean that an investor's decision of trading was wrong and selling a stock at a profit would mean that the investor took the right trade decision. Hence, the investor will be more willing to sell off those securities for which prices have risen than to sell those that will incur losses. But a good investor must get rid of a bad-performing asset at the quickest.

Of course, the loss or profit in trading is always taken against the purchase price of the security, which is a critical reference point. *This theory is pretty much in line with Prospect Theory, which states that losses prick twice as hard as the joy of gains.*

So, what are the implications of the disposition effect?

One of the most common implications is that the fear of loss makes investors disinvest often. But in reality, they would have been better off had they stayed invested longer. Thus, the disposition effect prevents investors from getting benefits of the stock price momentum.

To overcome this effect, an investor must choose to continually review his underperforming assets and consider selling them at the earliest.

Availability Bias

Availability bias refers to being biased towards readily available information. For example, the number of deaths each year in India is far more due to myocardial infarction (heart attacks) than car accidents. But when somebody dies in an accident, we hear about it on the news on TV and read about it plenty of times in newspapers. A survey was done recently to see what people state as the most common cause of deaths in India, and surprisingly, people chose road injuries as the biggest cause of deaths. This is a classic example of availability bias, as people have developed biases towards the available information.

How Can You Overcome Psychological Biases?

It is essential to overcome biases to arrive at the right decisions. Every one of us, whether an investor or a non-investor, is under the influence of one or many biases. But a successful investor or a businessman is one who has learnt to look beyond these biases.

Let us figure out ways to deal with behavioural biases.

1. *Look at the big picture:* The securities market is highly interlinked both at domestic as well as at global levels.

When you only look at your investments, your perspective of observing the stock market also gets reduced.

But when you see what is happening around you and closely watch the growing industries, industry players, etc., you see the realistic view of the market.

Investments are bound to fluctuate, especially in the short run, but when you learn to analyse the investment scenario, such fluctuations do not matter anymore.

As per the advice of Israeli psychologist and economist Daniel Kahneman, 'Investors must check the frequency at which they see how well their invested stocks are performing.'

The following questions will help you to overcome biases better.

a. What is the reason for considering a particular stock for investment?
b. What is the time horizon available to you for staying invested?
c. What are the expected returns after one year from this investment?
d. What is the risk of this stock on your overall portfolio?
e. What if the stock underperforms compared to your expectation? Will you still stay invested for a long time, or will you want to quit? Also, try to find the reason behind your chosen option.

2. *Rely less on what you see:* Avoid making a judgement by looking at the reports or trends shown prominently on all news channels. Instead, you must try to engage more in

reading about the industries or companies in which you want to invest or have already invested.

3. *Be knowledgeable:* The more you learn about stock investments, the lesser your decisions are affected by behavioural biases. Knowledge is by far the most reliable instrument that will help you master the game of stock investment. Of course, you cannot learn every aspect of it, but reading can add a lot to your investment skills.

4. *Follow a good mentor:* If you are entirely new to investing and don't know a thing about it, then it would be wise to follow an investment guru like Warren Buffett, Charlie Munger, Ben Graham, Peter Lynch, etc. It will help you overcome a lot of apprehensions and ignore the widespread misinterpretations of stock market investments.

5. *Look at stock investment as a business owner:* As we have discussed earlier, every investment you make in the stock market must be looked at from the owner's perspective. You need to consider yourself as the owner of the company, and then analyse what you will get out of your investment in the company.

6. *Review your biases periodically:* You need to review your preferences periodically with the investments that you were tempted to make under the influence of those biases.

Make a list of all the biases that you are a victim of, and also make a note of how the investments done under those biases are performing now.

It will be good learning for you if you add a list of top-performing stocks under your chosen sectors of business. You must keep tracking your investment against the benchmark investment that is performing the best in that particular industry. This practice will be an eye-opening activity for you that will help you see beyond your biases and act wisely in the future.

7. *Find someone who challenges your investment opinion all the time:* This is one of the most effective ways of checking your investment strategies. Encourage your spouse, parents, children, or any other family member or friend to act as the critic of all your investment ideas.

You and your critic must get involved in a healthy conversation where you have to defend your investment ideas against a contrary viewpoint. This exercise will help you clearly spot loopholes in your investment ideas.

Okay, now let's answer an interesting question: *What is the most commonly seen bias?*

Poll: Which of the following behavioural biases affects investment decision-making the most?

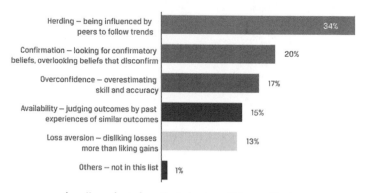

A poll conducted on the behavioural biases affecting investment decision-making

Source: CFA Institute, Financial News Brief

This survey involved 724 participants from across the globe. From the graph in Figure 16, it is clear that herding is the most common bias and accounts for 34 per cent of all biases.

21

Stock Investment Manifesto of Legendary Stock Investor Ben Graham

Famous American stock investor Ben Graham's investing principles are widely followed and looked up to across the globe. Graham's approach revolved around analysing the financial statements of the company. He believed that everything about a company could be known by analysing its financial statements.

Unfortunately, the quantitative factors do not cover all the aspects of investing. Nevertheless, here are some of the vital contributions of Benjamin Graham in the field of value investing.

The three concepts—Margin of safety, Mr Market, and Cigar butt approach—are the founding principles of investing, based on which we will study everything else. Let's understand them one by one.

Benjamin Graham's principles of investing

Margin of Safety

'A margin of safety is achieved when securities are purchased at prices sufficiently below underlying value to allow for human error, bad luck, or extreme volatility in a complex, unpredictable, and rapidly changing world.'

—Seth Klarman, value investor

Margin of Safety

The concept of margin of safety was first introduced by Graham, Warren Buffett's tutor, from whom Buffett learnt most of his investing skills.

The margin of safety is a principle that states that an investor wisely invests in those securities where the current listed price of the stock is lower than its intrinsic value. The intrinsic value of the stock is the fair value that is arrived at after the fundamental valuation of the stock is done.

The investment world is highly volatile and is subject to errors, unexpected events, or bad luck. In such cases, the margin of safety provides a great deal of protection and comfort to the investors.

Let's take an example. If you want to build an aircraft that can carry a weight of 100 kg at a time, you will instead make an aircraft that can carry 150 kg of weight but allow only 100 kg on a single flight. Here, the excess weight-bearing capacity of 50 kg is the margin of safety.

There are two reasons why you must consider the margin of safety:

1. The intrinsic value calculation of the stock may not always be correct. As humans, we are bound to make errors. So, choosing a share with a price below the intrinsic value gives an excellent safety for the investment.
2. The future of the market is highly unpredictable. Thus, a reasonable deal invites greater security!

Mr Market

Mr Market loves to fly high in the sky! He goes up and up and flies freely. Whoosh! The very next moment, you see him toppling down to hit the ground. You are stumped at what happened! But worry not, this is Mr Market's nature, to keep you entertained with his roller-coaster ride.

So, when Mr Market is flying high, you must enjoy the ride by selling overpriced stocks, but when Mr Market is sinking, you must buy good stocks.

Cigar Butt Approach

Have you seen cigar butts lying on the streets? Those butts are used, discarded, and dirty but can still give you the joy of that last puff. Of course, you get to enjoy it only if you have the guts to pick up a dirty cigar butt.

The same analogy has been used by Benjamin Graham to describe the negatively performing companies whose stocks have tumbled to become so cheap that they are as good as free cigar butts on the street.

Such stocks are dirt cheap and provide a golden chance to smart investors to invest in them. Of course, there is a lot of negativity and underperformance attached to these stocks, which creates a panic in the market. But for smart investors, it is a golden ticket to invest and reap huge benefits in the future.

To summarize, the cigar butt approach of investment suggests that you invest in the stock while keeping a considerable margin of safety, which provides a great deal of coverage to you at all times. When you invest in such low-performing stocks, you still don't lose anything; if the company liquidates, the liquidation value of each stock will be much higher than your current purchase value.

22

Learning to Invest in Stocks

Peter Lynch is considered a great stock investment guru and has one of the best track records as a mutual fund manager. He is known as one of the most influential personalities behind the concept of value investing. Let's understand his investment model to understand value investing better.

Avoid hot stocks in hot industries
—Peter Lynch

The Peter Lynch Model of Picking Stocks

This chapter is crucial to understanding the world of investing broadly. It introduces you to the key aspects of stock investment, and they will help you in a big way in understanding the indicators of good stocks.

It will be interesting to read these guidelines, which build the right intent to approach stock investment. Let us discuss these guidelines one by one.

Buy Simple Businesses

A word of caution for you: Never buy a business that you don't understand. Please remember that you can't value businesses that you don't understand. Let's evaluate this through a concept referred to as the 'circle of competence.'

Circle of Competence

The circle of competence is a popular concept devised by the guru of stock market investment, Warren Buffett. In one of his letters to the shareholders of Berkshire Hathaway in 1996, Buffett wrote:

> What an investor needs is the ability to correctly evaluate selected businesses. Note the word 'selected': You don't have to be an expert on every company or even many. You only have to be able to evaluate companies within your circle of competence. The size of that circle is not very important; knowing its boundaries, however, is vital.

In simple words, the circle of competence refers to areas in which we have enough knowledge through experience or studies.

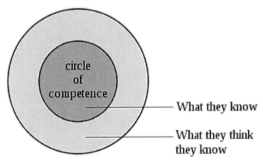

Euler diagram depicting the circle of competence

As per this concept, an investor must carefully select the stocks of those companies that he understands well. This is like a doctor knowing which drug or which pharmaceutical company is doing well. The doctor will even know the ethics of that pharma company. He will also be aware of the drugs that the company will launch soon. So, in short, a doctor knows and understands pharma companies a lot better than others. Hence, the probability of picking up good stocks of pharma companies is the highest in the case of a doctor.

But, if a doctor chooses to pick up stocks of a microchip company or an electrical goods company, then he is more likely to make investments based on the external perception of the companies. Here, stock picking will be based on superficial knowledge, which invites a high possibility of making mistakes.

As Warren Buffett puts it,

> *It is imperative to identify companies dealing in your core competency areas and start with investing in them. Though the circle will be extremely narrow when you start investing, it can widen over time slowly. It has been observed that people tend to make more mistakes in picking stocks when they stray from this discipline.*

Most successful businesspeople identify the perimeter of their circle of competence and operate inside it. Of course, over time, they keep working hard to build their knowledge and competence in new areas in which they venture in due course with sufficient knowledge.

One important thing to note about the circle of competence is that it is not the size or the number of businesses you target, but rather about how well you understand the business you have chosen. If you think your knowledge is restricted to just one area, then it is better to start investing money only in that one business. Slowly, as you build experience and exposure to other businesses, then you must consider investing in them.

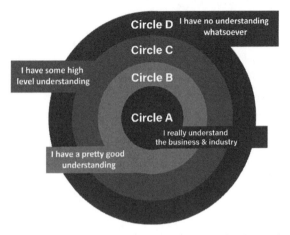

The circle of competence in relation to the level of understanding

Using Figure 18, your investment target should be companies falling in circle A, the innermost circle. Please note that the size of circle A does not matter at all; what matters is that you must never cross this circle. Besides, you must simultaneously keep working on those companies that fall in circle B.

Over the years, you will learn enough about the companies in circle B, and then you will have more opportunities to invest. But for creating wealth in stock investment, a few assured picks are far better than putting your interest in many stocks.

So, from this concept, the following should be straightforward and clear:

- If you are a doctor, invest in pharma companies.
- If you are an engineer, pick up tech stocks.

- If you are a biotechnologist, pick up pharma stocks.
- If you are an architect, pick up heavy industry stocks.

The key takeaway here is that you must not get confused when I say invest in companies that you understand well. You don't need to hold a degree or be a master analyser to follow these companies. Even an average investor can understand companies with focused research and efforts.

Note: The width of an investor's area of competence can be defined by his spending habits, the types of products he generally uses, and his profession.

According to Lynch, our biggest research tools are our eyes, ears, and common sense. If you find something fishy about the company, it is best to avoid it, as there cannot be just one cockroach in the sink. We buy dozens of things every week, so if something attracts you as a consumer, that's a good starting point to begin reading about that company as a potential investor.

Look for Boring Companies in Not So Exciting Industries

Let us take the example of Bitcoin (cryptocurrency) to understand whether investments should be boring or exciting. Bitcoin is by far the most successful cryptocurrency in the world. For those who don't know, a cryptocurrency is a virtual currency that uses cryptography for security. Bitcoin picked up considerable momentum due to its high volatility inviting large price fluctuations.

It is loved by investors who are high-risk-oriented and believe in being speculative to make quick, substantial gains.

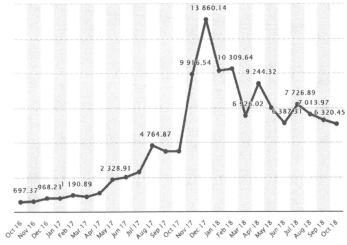

Bitcoin price index from October 2016 to October 2018 (in US$)

As you can see from the graph, the Bitcoin value started at US$ 697.37 in October 2016, reached US$ 13,860.14, and dropped to US$6,320 in October 2018. So, you can see the stark variation in the price of Bitcoin, which is why it has become so popular.

Likewise, people like to trade in stocks because they find it exciting to see the stock prices rising, which enables them to make money. But volatility is never a measure to define your success in stock investment, as we have already seen that any volatile commodity which has risen to an enjoyable hike takes a steep fall in the next moments due to its instability. Hence, stock traders who believe in chasing highly volatile stocks are often left disappointed, as the prices fluctuate highly with no substantial gains in the longer run.

So, if your targeted investments appear to be boring, you are on the right track. If the investments seem to be exciting, you need to reconsider your strategy of investment.

Lean towards Slow-Changing Industries

A good investor always welcomes change, but the change in the industry must be slow and relevant. Although the industry is bound to change, the ethics, motivation, and basic intent of the industry must remain the same.

From an investor's point of view, let us look at the following examples.

Companies like Coca-Cola have hardly changed themselves over the years. Coca-Cola has managed to grow multifold and currently enjoys a dominant market position. Such companies serve as an ideal investment option, as the dynamics of running the company have sustained over the years, and the strategies of running these companies have been successfully proven.

On the other hand, fast-changing companies like Nokia, Blackberry, and Kodak gained a lot of popularity but were quickly kicked out of business. They lost huge market shares as they missed a few cycles of change to launch newer versions of their latest products. Of course, it is exceptionally challenging to innovate new viable products every few months. It is obvious that companies that require such high levels of innovation to compete will eventually die out someday.

The moral of the story is that as an investor, look for companies that evolve and change but do so relatively slowly compared to fast-changing companies like Nokia, Blackberry, etc.

Figure Out 'The Inevitables'

Companies that are backed by solid management and have remained ethical in their approach are bound to bounce back successfully, defying all odds. Such companies are called 'the inevitables' by Warren Buffett. Let's look at two examples, the first of which is Coca-Cola.

Long back, Coca-Cola diversified to launch a new variant called Cherry Coke, which didn't go as they expected. Of course, a lot of funds were required to research, launch, and promote Cherry Coke. Unfortunately, this new product did not do as well as hoped and had to be called off. Coca-Cola suffered huge losses, which resulted in delayed returns to the stock investors. But eventually, investing in Coca-Cola did pay off, and investors were able to get good returns on their investments.

The lesson this teaches us here is that a loss of focus may happen temporarily to good companies because every company goes through a learning phase. Most importantly, every learning in business either brings you profits or an invaluable experience to grow and develop further.

The second example is that of Gillette. A few decades back, Gillette, the market leader in the blade industry, thought of diversifying its business. It started exploring oil aggressively but failed miserably in it. Expanding into oil exploration cost it heftily, but still, Gillette could sail through the losses smoothly as it was the market leader in the blade industry with a 60 per cent market share. It could easily bounce back with consistent profit inflow and eventually pay off very high dividends to its investors.

Be Patient as an Investor

One of the important things to note is that as an individual investor, you must go slow in choosing stocks. Take ample time to read and gather information about your preferred companies, and always remember that haste makes waste.

Small Investments Do Matter!

As a small investor, you may wonder how you will earn satisfactory returns by investing a small amount of money. You may believe that by buying a few shares, nothing substantial can be gained. But even a few right investments can fetch much bigger returns with the power of compounding.

Interesting Information on the Psychology of an Individual Investor

A common fear that a small investor has is that he may have little chance of survival in the stock market as compared to pro-investors. Often, it is believed that big influential investors like renowned businessmen or celebrities have direct access to a company's inside information, as they know the top officials of the company very well. So, people think these influential investors can take advantage of the information revealed secretly to them and act accordingly to fetch immense returns.

But the fact is that the inside information available to influential people might not be correct at all times, as even big companies hire highly skilled sales professionals to plant a good image of the company in the minds of influential, big investors. Any information that is planted does not act in the best interests of investors.

On the contrary, small investors must be happy that they are away from this intended manipulation. They are free to place bets based on the ethical evaluation of the businesses, which invites much higher chances of success.

Never Believe the Advice That You Read or Hear

As an individual investor, always try to dig deeper to understand a company before investing in it. You must never blindly believe the advice that you get to read in the newspaper or hear on news channels.

Choose the Growing Companies in India

Identify the growing companies in India and invest in them as a long-term investor to get hefty returns in the future. But, as Warren Buffett states, if you are not willing to own a stock for 10 years, then don't own it even for 10 minutes.

This is one of the suggestions that you must always keep in mind. Individual investors like Warren Buffett grew to become multi-billionaires just by taking the right approach to investment.

Latest Quarterly Reports Don't Tell the Entire Story

Most investors try to gauge a company's performance by checking its latest quarterly published report. In reality, these reports give a snapshot of the most recent quarterly performance of the company, which can be misleading.

Such reports work if you are trading in stocks to target short-term earnings. Quarterly reports do not tell anything about the long-term survival of the company, nor do they talk about the management practices of the company. So, one cannot make out anything about the company's prospects just by looking at its current report, even though it might look promising.

Go for Businesses that Focus on a Niche Market

Companies with focused niches are easier to target than others. For example, a company X may be manufacturing five different products, A, B, C, D, and E. Suppose only A outperforms, and the other products don't. But the consolidated annual report of the company shows positive growth indicating good profits. So, as an investor, you might get tempted to invest in it! But can you rely on the future of the company, and on how long a single product can overshadow four other underperforming products?

Hence, as a convention, any company that is into multiple businesses must reveal a separate business report for each of its businesses. But from an investor's view, it gets complicated to understand the performance of such companies. Hence, it would be wiser to avoid such companies, at least in the initial learning stages.

Check Business Ethics

The negative growth of a company should be reported as promptly as a positive one. A company cannot keep outperforming at all times and cannot show higher cash inflows too. A company may not incur losses but may have made substantial investments to expand or diversify, which must reflect in its cash outflow, and must be revealed as is in the annual report.

Look for a Proportionate Increase in Stock Value

According to seasoned investors, theorists, and fundamentalists, the stock price must appreciate such that for every Re 1 retained by the company, the shareholder must earn Re 1. For example, if a company chooses to retain Rs 100 from the profits and does not give it away as dividends, then the shareholders' wealth must eventually rise by Rs 100.

Beware of Companies Making Too Many Predictions

Beware of the company that makes too many positive predictions, as it is a bad management practice. There is no surety of such predictions turning true! And it surely manipulates the behaviour of market buyers, sellers, and brokers, which is not ethical. And of course, such companies may not be ethical on various fronts as they have already compromised on their ethics here.

Also, *beware of the companies that claim to have been consistently performing at or above the declared targets.* Remember that no company can always meet declared targets or exceed them for several years. There is a high possibility of the data being made up here.

Look for Prospering Industries

If a company is into multiple businesses, then not all its businesses will increase its profits. Of course, a company's growth is directly dependent on the growth of the industry. But when the industry suffers setbacks, the same may get reflected in the company's performance after a while.

Usually, if the company's management is competent, it works hard to minimize the ill effects of the industry. This may prolong the latent period for the losses to show up for the company. So, as an investor, you need to look at industries that have positive growth potential in the future. Let us understand this with an example.

Warren Buffett had invested in the textile business long back. He was incredibly blessed to have a great, dedicated team of labourers and managers who could handle work very efficiently.

The textile industry was struggling to mark its existence in those days. But Buffett did not feel the negative influence of the industry on his business, because his efficient team kept performing well to minimize the ill effects of the industry on the business.

Eventually, the business had to be shut as the industry itself was in its darkest phase. Consequently, Buffett suffered enormous losses, for he had invested heavily in that business. So, a good management team can overshadow the effects of adverse market influences. If the team had not worked so efficiently, then Warren Buffett would have shut this business long back, and undoubtedly incurred much fewer losses.

The moral of the story is that stocks of promising ventures may give mediocre returns if the industry is not performing well, but the same stocks can fetch better returns if the sector does well.

Remember, the Intrinsic Value Increases Early

A company's intrinsic value rises at a faster pace compared to market recognition of its success.

As soon as the news of any new business expansion is out, the positive effect is seen on the share prices. It should be noted that even though the company has not started earning additional revenue yet, the intrinsic value starts soaring.

Follow the Investment Principle

The true underlying principle of value investing is that 'investors gain as the market goes down.' In reality, only dis-investors lose as the market goes down because when the market is down, it's time to buy more shares of promising companies at a lower price.

Avoid Making Decisions Based on Predictions

Nobody ever has, had, and will have any idea about where the stock market will be a year later. Hence, you must avoid making any decisions based on predictions that you hear or read.

Follow a Good Strategy

The investment market is ideal as long as the investor sticks to a sound investment strategy. A good investment strategy seldom fails!

Invest Wisely

Never buy a mediocre business at a bargain price. Always put your brain to the test while picking up a low-priced stock.

Analyse the Company's Present Worth

Analysing businesses does not require any technical knowledge to understand beta profits or to decode the modern portfolio theory, speculate efficient markets, look for option pricing or emerging markets, etc. It just needs a detailed eye, patience, and skill to analyse a company's present worth.

Stock Split

Some companies opt to split their high-priced stocks to attract investors. But the stock split of top-priced shares does no good. This is because the companies attract non-value investors who speculate, which results in price swings.

Understand the Investment Motives of a Company

The investment motives of the top management must be coupled with the right investment price. For example, it is always wise to buy 10 per cent ownership of a promising company at a price of Rs X per share, rather than acquiring it 100 per cent at a price of Rs 2X per share.

Mergers and Acquisitions

Most companies acquire other companies only to satiate their ego. While many companies believe that through acquisition their efficient management will turn an average-performing company into an over-performing one, this is not always true!

The management must instead make acquisitions for the following reasons:

a. The acquired company has the potential to grow further.
b. The acquired company has the technical know-how that will help the acquiring company gain a competitive advantage.
c. The acquired company is available at a cheap valuation.

The biggest challenge that comes with the acquisition of a company is to be fair to the shareholders of both companies.

Working Capital Status

A spurt in debtors and inventory of a company indicates that it is facing working capital issues. It is an important metric of financial liquidity, business efficiency, and the overall operations of the company. Thus, inefficient working capital management will lead to financial trouble, the sale of fixed assets, and even the shutting down of business operations.

A piece of advice for new investors is that they must invest in touch-and-feel kind of businesses where they can understand the value of the products by using them. Examples include Gillette and Colgate.

Note: The research on the points discussed above brings in a lot of confidence in you as an investor. Your small seeds of investments, if placed rightly, have the potential to grow into immense wealth over the years. Hence, this research is a must-do for long-term investment returns.

23

Who Is My Well-Wisher in the Stock Market?

You must have read that the hardcore bitter reality of the stock market is that 'nobody is your well-wisher.' Yes, you read it right!

Although there are plenty of stock advisors or brokers to help you in making investments, they are all working for their profits first. They don't care about your investments; all they care about is the fat commissions they receive from their suggested investments.

Figure 20 shows the participants who act as advisors in the stock market.

Figure 20: Various stock market advisors

Now, let us see the hidden facts behind the advice of each of these advisors.

Brokers

Brokers advise you to buy or sell a stock and earn a brokerage fee out of it. They make money via commissions earned by buying or selling shares. So, they advise you to invest in those funds from which they can earn a hefty brokerage fee.

Generally, brokers give five different types of ratings to investors, which are: *buy, accumulate, hold, underweight, and sell.*

From personal experience, here is what the broker's ratings mean.

Sell: The brokers are required to be on good terms with the CEOs of the companies, and hence, the brokers refrain from suggesting selling.

Underweight: This is their softer way to suggest selling.

Hold: This means that you must start selling the stocks, as they do not appear to be promising to the broker anymore.

Accumulate: This means holding the stocks.

Buy: The brokers usually have to meet their monthly brokerage targets by facilitating more transactions through stock recommendations. So 'buy' does not assure that the stock is worthy of being bought.

Credit Rating Agencies

It is not recommended that you invest your money based on the credit ratings given by rating agencies, as you can be misguided. Here's how.

Companies are dependent on the ratings of these agencies for fundraising, and hence, they offer the agencies hefty commissions to obtain good ratings. Consequently, the ratings presented by these credit rating agencies can be misleading.

Advisors

Every year, advisors need to make the research reports of companies, which requires them to meet the companies' senior officials frequently. So, they need to take special care of these top officials' interests in order to retrieve the financial data from them. Thus, in short, advisors' ratings are always manipulated to show the companies as excellent investment opportunities.

Mutual Fund Distributors

Even mutual fund distributors work for their selfish reasons. They suggest only those funds that will give them maximum returns.

Relationship Advisors in the Bank

When you visit your bank, you often ask your relationship manager (RM) which insurance policy or stock market fund you should invest in. And you will find your RM instantly suggesting a few policies and a few funds with a lot of conviction. But beware. Your RM will only indicate the policy, scheme, or fund from which he earns the maximum commission. The RMs or other sales staff of financial institutions are paid both in-kind and cash to promote the sale of a specific scheme or a fund.

So, imagine! If by selling an X fund, your RM is sent on a free trip to Singapore, and by selling a Y fund, he is sent to Dubai, and suppose he wishes to go to Dubai, then he will present the Y fund as a better investment option as compared to X!

Sadly, this hardcore reality has existed in the financial market for a long time. The poor investors are used as bait to earn the brokerage commission from trading or to get a commission from the companies.

Tip: You must get involved in stock investment yourself by learning the very basics of how to select the right stocks. It may be a little time-taking, but it is certainly not difficult. I believe that by the end of this book, you will be equipped with the right knowledge and tools to assess stocks by yourself.

An interesting thought to ponder over here is, *'Why is it important to give 100 per cent honest advice in the financial sector?'*

Financial advice plays a critical role in defining huge gains or losses for an investor. With one right financial advice, an investor can mint multi-billions, and with one wrong advice, he loses the golden opportunity to create such enormous wealth.

When it comes to other areas, the loss is limited to the wrong advice that has been given. For example, if you buy a faulty car, scooter, or property based on the advice of a professional advisor, then the loss is restricted to just a car or a scooter or a property.

But in the case of financial advice related to stock investment, the loss can be unlimited. Think about it. You want to buy a share X that is worth Rs 100, and you seek a financial advisor's help. He advises not to invest in X's share, and instead suggests some other share Y. Out of confusion, you forgo the opportunity to invest money in either of the shares.

After 10 years, share X's value appreciated to Rs 50,000. Suppose you had intended to buy ten shares of X. It would have fetched you Rs 5 lakh. But because of the wrong advice of the broker, you lost out on this excellent opportunity. Thus, the loss is enormous due to the power of compounding.

So, being a financial advisor is a huge responsibility, as with one piece of advice, an investor can either create enormous wealth or incur huge losses. Hence, you should choose a financial advisor who has ethics and integrity.

Now let me give you an interesting insight.

Beware! Often, things that are too big to fail are covered up!

As citizens of India, we have faith in the Indian public sector banks, and we seek their help and guidance in planning our financial investments, right? But the reality is that with public sector undertakings, the picture is not as good as it looks.

There have been a few massive scams perpetrated by big financial institutions in the past. A lot of noise was made to highlight these scams, but no legal actions were taken against the banks.

A report released by RBI for 2017–2018 states that public sector banks accounted for 92.9 per cent of the amount involved in scams, whereas private sector banks accounted for only 6 per cent.

Here are some graphs giving a clear picture of the fraudulence reported by public sector banks in the past:

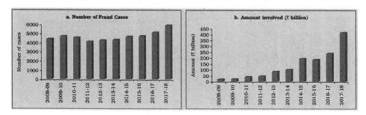

Graph showing the number of fraud cases between 2008 and 2018 and the amounts involved

Source: RBI Supervisory Returns

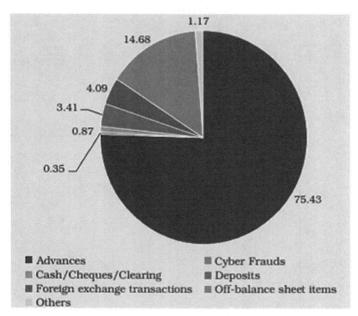

Pie chart showing the various types of frauds

Source: RBI Supervisory Returns

Frauds on the part of the governmental financial institutions were shocking.

Public sector units or PSUs ate away crores of rupees in a scam that went viral. But the government, instead of taking any legal action against the PSUs, recapitalized the public banks and charged hefty taxes from citizens to make up for the losses.

Do you know why? It is because PSUs are *too big to fail*. Now let's see what this 'too big to fail' theory is.

The 'Too Big to Fail' Theory

Certain financial institutions are so well integrated into the Indian economy that their failures would devastate a significant portion of the economic system. Hence, for the economic welfare of the country, the government is bound to support such institutions when they face any significant failures.

Here is an example of what happens if 'too big to fail' institutions fail.

SBI has around 22,500 branches and 58,000 ATMs. The total asset value of SBI is Rs 37 lakh crore, which is more than US$ 555 billion. There are more than 50 crore Indian customers who have put their faith in SBI by saving money in it.

So, if at any time SBI is dissolved, the money invested in crores will be doomed, leading to significant economic devastation. It will crash the Indian economy at once. Therefore, such institutions are named 'too big to fail.'

Currently, SBI is planning to increase its market share to 22 per cent from 17 per cent, owing to the growing demand for public banks in India. So, it will be even more difficult to legally dissolve this institution in the future, as this will mean the failure of the government of India. So these institutions continue to flourish; but the good news is that they have mended their ways due to the entry of foreign banking companies.

Currently, three banks have been recognized by RBI as 'too big to fail' banks: SBI, ICICI Bank, and HDFC Bank.

24

The Fallacian Trap

A Self-Proposed Theory

The Fallacian Trap is one of my self-devised theories, which is inspired by common fraudulent practices seen in the investment industry.

Stock brokerage companies indulge in scams that I call *The Fallacian Trap*. These scams target the people who fall for fancy schemes or plans. The brokerage companies mint money out of the folly of these innocent people.

To understand this scam, let us take a look at the following example. A brokerage company pulls out the contact details of 1,000 people randomly and divides them into two groups, say, Group A and Group B. Each group contains 500 people.

To *Group A*, the company says Reliance shares will rise in price (this is just an example). To *Group B*, the company says Reliance shares will drop in price.

Now, let's assume that owing to market fluctuations, the price of shares hiked. So, the 500 people falling in Group A gained faith in the stock brokerage firm, as the stock prices behaved as predicted by the firm. On the contrary, Group B lost faith in the company, and the company shifted its focus to Group A now.

Again, the 500 people in Group A are divided into two groups, say *Group 'a'* and *Group 'b'*. Each group now has 250 people in it. Now, once again, the stock advisory company tells Group 'a' that the prices will hike, and it tells Group 'b' that the prices will fall. Now, suppose the prices for *Group 'a'* are hiked again. So, the faith of *Group 'a'* in the company is bolstered, and *Group 'b'* loses faith in it.

The company further divides the remaining 250 people into two different groups and repeats the same process. The handful of people remaining at the end has tested the company's stock price predictions several times and gained confidence in the company's investment advisory skills. This is the most vulnerable set of people for the Fallacian Trap.

The stock advisory firm now shares tempting investment schemes to trap the final filtered set of people. These schemes usually act as a trap for innocent people who lose their money later.

This is how innocent investors like you and me fall for the trap. In the financial world, everyone is out for their gains first. But you're lucky to have found out about such loopholes through this book!

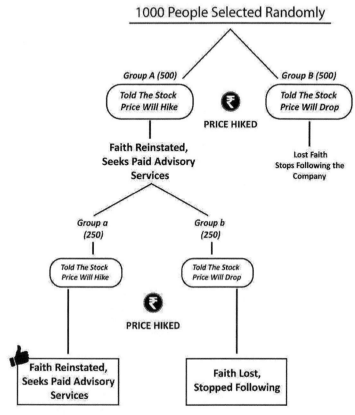

Diagrammatic representation of the Fallacian Trap

25

How Many Stocks Must You Own?

By now, you have read the basics of stock market investment and the rules or guidelines that can help you create successful ventures that fetch high returns. But after having read so much about how to invest, the fundamental question remains: *'How many stocks should I own to have a significant investment portfolio?'*

If you too had this question in your mind all this while, don't worry! You are not alone in looking for an answer to this.

In earlier days, investments in stocks were guided by modern management theory. As per the theory, investors are taught to 'never lay all the eggs in one basket.' Rather, they should look at diversifying their portfolio to diversify the risk. But nowadays, a concentrated investment portfolio is considered a better bet than a diversified one.

Today, it is believed that an investor must lay all his eggs in one basket and watch that basket grow. This concept is believed and followed by all investment gurus worldwide.

This is because the idea of value investing has replaced the concept of diversified investment that prevailed earlier.

So, any investment that you make today should be well-researched and based on the valuation of the company. If the stocks are selected with this approach, it is evident that only a few stocks will fit the specifications, and hence, the portfolio will be concentrated.

Warren Buffett emphasizes that you must measure every investment wisely and invest with an attitude that it is the only investment you will ever make. And by following this practice, you will have fewer stocks but a well-thought-out, well-researched investment portfolio. But the question still remains: How many stocks should you opt for in the beginning?

Here is what the famous legends suggest on buying stocks.

The best way to get into investment is to buy stocks within your circle of competence. You must pick one or two companies that you think are in a business that you understand well. Try to delve deeper and find out more about those companies by digging into the details discussed in earlier chapters. Keep repeating the same process with other securities. Slowly, you will keep adding to your portfolio to increase the number of investments.

So, it is good to have a well-thought-out collection of stocks in your portfolio, but coming to a specific number will be difficult. Most professional investors stick to keeping 15 to 20 stocks in their investment portfolio as a thumb rule. Ben Graham indicates that any number of shares between 10 and 30 is good enough to have a stable, risk-averse portfolio. In contrast, Warren Buffett advises restricting your collection to just 5 to 10 stocks.

But if you still want to know what the ideal number of stocks to hold in a portfolio is, then there is no consensus on this.

As per my advice, when you start as an investor, you will tend to make mistakes, so you should diversify your portfolio rather than betting on one or two stocks. Of course, if you are young with no dependents, then you can buy more stocks depending on your disposable income.

There are two kinds of risks that an investor is exposed to over time. One is called 'unsystematic risk,' which is associated with the company or industry you have invested in. The other is 'systematic risk,' which indicates the risk of the entire stock market crashing or a recession. Having more stocks in a portfolio, guards you against the unsystematic risk to a great extent. And by being a serious long-term investor, you guard against the systematic risk of investment anyway.

Good Stocks Defy All Odds

The stocks of companies with efficient management defy all odds and tend to perform very well in the long run.

When there was a stock market crash in India between 1992 and 2003, the Sensex hit an all-time low, but stocks of good companies like Infosys still moved up a few thousand times. Besides, other stocks of some promising companies in the technology, pharmaceuticals, and FMCG sectors also moved up considerably during this crash. This shows that good stocks end up delivering good results during the negative years too, provided you hold on to them for a longer time.

Stocks or Mutual Funds: Which Is a Better Investment Bet?

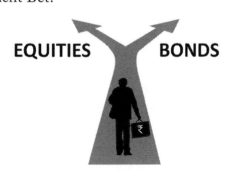

The biggest myth that has been around for decades is that mutual fund investors have a safer ride compared to individual investors. But is this true? Let's dig deeper to understand who is at an advantage when it comes to stock investment.

For decades, mutual fund investments have been believed to be a safe bet in stock investment. Yet individual investments are considered better than mutual fund investments.

Can Individual Investors Outperform the Mutual Fund Investors?

Yes, individual investors can outperform mutual fund investors at times due to the following reasons:

1. *Risk-taking ability:* The fund managers cannot take the risk as they are accountable for someone else's money, so they have to play safe. On the other hand, individual investors can take as much risk as they want because they invest their own money.

For example, suppose a fund manager invested his client's money to buy a few stocks of Infosys Ltd. But due to market fluctuations, Infosys' stock price drops, leading to a loss. In this case, the fund manager is usually not blamed for the losses, as Infosys is considered one of the safest bets for investment. Any investor will blindly invest money in big names like Infosys. On the other hand, if the same fund manager had invested in a stock like V2 Retail, and if its prices had dropped, his investment skills and understanding would be questioned, as V2 is an unpopular stock.

So, mutual fund managers are forced to refrain from taking a risk to protect their image and keep their jobs secure.

2. *SEBI regulations:* A mutual fund company is bound by SEBI regulations, unlike an individual investor. As per SEBI, a mutual fund company has to abide by the following guidelines:

- A fund manager cannot invest more than 10 per cent of total assets under management in one stock, whereas an individual investor has 100 per cent freedom of investment.
- A large-cap fund cannot invest in a small company, whereas an individual investor can invest anywhere at any time as per his wish.
- A mutual fund has serious liquidity concerns to liquidate the generated portfolio. On the contrary, an individual investor can liquidate his stocks as freely as required.
- A mutual fund manager cannot choose when to sell the stocks. He has to sell the stocks when redemption pressure crops in, but an individual investor faces no such

challenge. The same has been explained with an example later.

- A mutual fund company cannot invest because of its huge financial investment corpus and due to the SEBI disclosure requirement, but an individual investor is not bound by any such regulation.

Sounds complicated, right? Let's understand this with an example. Suppose an XYZ company has released 1,000 shares at Rs 100 each. The mutual fund company sees potential in XYZ company and wants to purchase a vast number of its shares. Also, the mutual fund company is aware that XYZ will release the next 1,000 shares later.

Suppose the mutual fund company bought all 1,000 shares at Rs 100. So, as per SEBI guidelines, any investment of more than 10 per cent needs to be disclosed publicly. Thus, the next day's newspaper will reveal that so and so mutual fund company has bought 1,000 shares of XYZ. As soon as this news is out, the price of the stocks of XYZ company will increase as the demand has increased.

After this, XYZ releases another 1,000 shares at a hiked price of say Rs 500. Now the mutual fund company will be reluctant to buy a new set of 1,000 stocks, as the prices have increased. This is how a mutual fund company is not able to buy enough quantities of stocks because of its vast corpus and SEBI disclosure requirement.

Now, let me share with you a personal experience depicting how individual investment outperforms most of the time.

A couple of years back, one of my family friends sought advice from me on stock investment. I had researched a company that appeared to have a promising future. I bought a few of its shares and advised my friend to buy some. The shares were priced at Rs 500 at the time we both bought them.

After a few weeks, the share price dropped to Rs 400, and my friend started worrying. But since I had faith in the company, I bought a few more shares at a reduced price and advised my friend to buy some more. My friend reluctantly purchased a few more shares on my advice. After some time, the prices dropped to Rs 300, and he again sought my opinion on this investment.

I insisted that he hold on to those shares and also advised him to buy more, as I did. He still bought some more shares but very hesitantly. Finally, the prices dropped to Rs 200 a few days later. My investor friend lost belief in me and sold off all the shares at a massive loss of 60 per cent. But I continued to buy more shares of that company as I knew the prices would bounce back soon. Now, my average price per share became Rs 210. In three years, the stock price increased to Rs 700 and I made three times my initial investment value.

So, as an individual investor, I could take the risk with my money and so, acted as per my wish, thus made good money. But as an advisor, my hands were tied, and the funds had to be liquidated against my will when the redemption pressure cropped in. As I said earlier, patience usually pays off in the stock market if the fundamentals are strong.

26

Bagging the Multi-Bagger Stocks!

You will often come across the term 'multi-bagger stocks' in newspapers or on financial news channels. Let's understand the real concept behind this new buzzword.

Multi-bagger stocks are stocks that fetch huge returns at multiple times the initial investment costs. Such stocks generate not just huge profits but tremendous wealth to let you live life king-size.

It is due to multi-bagger stocks that stock investment expert and the ideal of many, Warren Buffett, created his multi-billion worth. He was fortunate enough to have chosen the multi-bagger stocks at the right time.

How can you pick the multi-bagger stocks?

1. *Identify a company that sells in mass volumes and has premium margins. The stocks of such companies prove to be multi-bagger stocks.*

A company can either compromise between selling in volumes or earning great margins. It is very difficult for a company to excel in both these business models. Maruti, for instance, is known for selling in volumes, whereas Mercedes is known for earning huge margins.

Here are a few examples of multi-bagger companies that have excelled in selling in huge numbers at premium prices.

- Foreign companies: Starbucks, Apple, etc.
  Apple products are the costliest with respect to their competitors, and yet Apple's products are able to land in the hands of almost every other household. This is only possible because of its unique design and customer-friendly interface. People are loyal towards the brand, and its stickiness is such that they always (mostly) come back to its products.

- Domestic companies: Eicher Motors, Page Industries (Jockey Brand Innerwear), etc.
  Royal Enfield Bullet, manufactured by Eicher Motors, is sold in huge volumes at a very high price. *Why?* Well, the bike's model and engine have never been updated in the last many years. The beauty of the model lies in its nostalgia. Without any drastic upgradation of features

or change in design and style, the Bullet is the highest selling bike of Eicher Motors.

The stocks of these companies have multiplied over 100 times in the last 10 years, making them multi-bagger stocks.

2. *Scan the environment.* Find out the track record of the management of the company. How has the company been performing in the past? What are the future growth prospects of the industry? You must try to gather all such necessary details about the company before investing in it.
3. *Is the company benefiting from a passing trend, or is its competitive advantage sustainable?*

Never invest in companies that are temporarily benefiting from a change of policy or any other external environmental factor, as you will lose your money soon when the company loses the benefits of the passing trend.

A real-life example of this is the graphite industry in India. Back in November 2018, China introduced a policy ban on steel mills to check the pollution caused by the rising level of smog. So, China started importing graphite from countries like India to satisfy its manufacturing needs. As a result, India's graphite industry started seeing an upsurge, resulting in stock price hikes of companies like Graphite India and HEG.

Later in 2019, the competition in the graphite industry rose, and then export to countries like China and Iran was curbed. So, the profit margins of Graphite India and HEG dropped drastically. Now, if as an investor you had picked up a stock of Graphite India, your money would have been at risk. The lesson here is to check if the company has sustainable profits or if it is just benefiting temporarily due to some favourable circumstances.

The Hunt for 100× Returns

The small-cap and mid-cap funds are looked upon as funds with high returns. But these funds come with their inherent risks, as there are many factors that influence these stock prices.

For example, a few years back, small-cap funds were considered the most promising investments, giving excellent returns to investors. But in the past year, small-cap funds have been suffering from huge losses and are still declining further in their prices.

27

A Bird's Eye View to Investing

Can you think of some exciting feature that interests a big investor? If you think hard, you can list down a couple of them. A prominent investor is always on the lookout for the right company to acquire, or a major stake in a well-performing company.

The most common measure of finding the true worth and size of the company is market capitalization, which refers to the total value of a company. This is analysed in the following way:

Market capitalization = Total number of shares × Price of one share

Let's assume a company X has 20,000 shares floating in the market. And the price of each share is, say, Rs 500. So, the market capitalization is:

Market capitalization = 20,000 × 500 = Rs 1,00,00,000

The Bird's Eye Perspective

An investor needs to be extremely aware of his ways of investing to make profitable investments. The more the investment value, the more careful the investor needs to be as he is putting a much higher value at stake.

Let's say you are planning to buy company X at the cost of Rs 1 crore. You need to do a proper cost-benefit analysis by first figuring out where else you can use the Rs 1 crore. This is to ensure that you evaluate every possible opportunity around you to make the best possible use of that Rs 1 crore.

Developing this perspective is essential if you want to place the right bets in the investment industry. Seasoned investors like Warren Buffett, Thomas Rowe Price Jr, John Neff, Jesse Livermore, Peter Lynch, and many more practice this strategy of finding the best available alternative before investing a considerable sum.

I strongly recommend this perspective as it helps you evaluate the true worth and value of your money. I want to remind you here once again that a wrong investment in stock, irrespective of its value, can cause you immense loss that's far bigger than the value invested. So, knowing the power of stock investment as a money multiplier, it becomes essential to evaluate available options or alternatives before investing a huge amount of money in a company.

28

An Essential Checklist for Stock Investments

The concepts in this book form a complete beginner's guide to investing in stocks. This chapter contains an overview of the book in the form of a checklist to narrow down your choices.

This checklist resonates with the best-proven principles of investment followed by Charlie Munger. Munger is the best investment advisor in the world and has shared the following principles in his book called *Poor Charlie's Almanack*.

These principles will provide the decisiveness you need to make safe, systematic investments that are factual and realistic.

1. *Understand the line of business.*
- Have you understood the company's business and the industry?
- Do you understand how this business makes money?
- How is the track record of the business so far?
- Have you checked to see that the industry does not have a high degree of obsolescence?

2. *How is the economy of the industry that you are willing to plunge in?*
- Do you think that the market for this business will grow substantially for another decade or so?
- Do you believe that the company will maintain a good ROE for the next 10 years or so?
- What is that one economic moat of the company that segregates it from the rest of the competitors?
- Can the business dictate price terms without losing out on customers?
- Are the exit barriers very low in cost that will allow a company to exit anytime it wants to?
- Is the business strong enough to dictate terms to its suppliers?
- How intense is the competition in this business?

3. *Understand the financial health of the company.*
- How is the current financial health of the company?
- Has the past decade witnessed consistent growth in sales and profit of the company?
- Does the company have a low debt-to-equity ratio (unless it's a financial institution or a bank)?
- Does the company have Foreign Currency Convertible Bonds (FCCB)? It is not mandatory for every company to have FCCB but having them brings credibility to the company.
- What is the current worth or total asset value of the company?
- Is the company able to earn a good amount of free cash flow? (The company might earn good profits every year as credit, which can get realized or can end up becoming a bad debt. Hence, free cash flow assures that the company has confirmed the availability of funds currently.)

4. *Take measured risks.*

You must always think before you leap when it comes to making financial investments. Hence, to take calculated risks, you must ensure the following:

- Keep a reasonable margin of safety
- Check the track record of the people, companies, or advisors you are dealing with.
- Avoid making hasty decisions.
- Don't be too aggressive. Sit back and think patiently.
- Keep a check on the changing market parameters such as inflation, government regulations, interest rate changes, etc.

5. *Have an independent approach.*

Never fall victim to herd mentality syndrome. Always use fundamental analysis and your judgement for making investments. Slowly, you will learn how to gauge the stocks and when to invest in them! This is a learning experience that will benefit you for a lifetime.

6. *Be a learner.*
- It is far more critical to approach investments in the right manner than to make the right investments.
- You need to learn, read, be curious, and be observant to learn the art of investment.
- Investing is a journey on the go; you need to become wiser with each passing day.
- You must have the habit of asking 'why' about everything you see around you to become a smart investor someday!

7. *Be humble and realistic.*
- You need to be modest and realistic in accepting what you don't know.
- Do not just make up your concepts and beliefs without having any solid underlying basis for them.
- You must take care to operate only within your circle of competence, no matter how small it is.

8. *Be analytical.*
- Look at the value of investment rather than just looking at its price.
- Look at the larger picture of a company that takes you beyond its worth, its current activity, and positioning. Try to see how it is trying to impact the lives of people.

- Always try to think forwards and backwards to analyse a business. You must aim at becoming a business analyst rather than a security analyst.

9. *Allocate your capital wisely.*
- The most critical thing for an investor is to allocate his capital wisely.
- Always remember that the term 'best investment' is relative and not absolute. So the 'best' is still defined by the second-best. Thus, the parameters defining the best investment keep changing all the time.
- Excellent investment options are hard to find. When you see a lot of odds stuck to a stock, it might be a great investment opportunity for you.
- Never get attached to any stock that favoured you in the past. Always look for opportunities and understand the market well.

10. *Be patient.*
- Never trade unnecessarily, or else you will only get to read about the immense power of compound interest and will never reap its benefits in reality.
- Learn to enjoy the process as it takes you to your destination. Enjoying the process hones your skills of investment.
- Never bear unnecessary transactional costs by being a mere trader.
- Always think, think, and think before acting.

11. *Take the right decisions.*
- Under all circumstances, you must be capable of analysing the factors correctly to arrive at the correct conclusions.

- The conclusions are highly time-dependent, and you need to have the conviction to choose wisely between the options.
- As per the general convention, you must do the opposite of what you see others doing. Be fearful of making investments when others are confident and vice-versa.
- A good investment policy is to keep your mind prepared at all times, to hear the good and the bad news—as the stock market is a highly fluctuating place—and keep your emotions aside while investing in stocks.

12. *Be ready to change.*
- Change is the only constant factor in life, and they say one must change as the world changes. Likewise, the rules of the game change with time, so you must embrace the new standards with grace and happiness. And you need to adapt to the changes in the world, as the world will never change as per your wishes.
- Deal with the bitter truths! It is a myth that truth is always painful; instead, it is far better than lies.

13. *Stay focused.*
- You must be simple in your investment approach and have simple expectations.
- Never get distracted by the trends to gamble or trade around.
- Be a serious investor and look at each business from the owner's perspective.
- It is always okay to make mistakes, but you need to avoid repeating the same mistakes.

- While analysing a stock, consider even the smallest unfavourable factor, as even a tiny hole in the ship can sink it.

14. *Evaluate stock pricing.*
- Is the stock of the company overpriced or under-priced as compared to its intrinsic value?
- Is the company expected to grow at a fast rate?
- Have you checked the P/E ratio? The P/E ratio tells how much money you are paying for every rupee of earnings. The P/E ratio gives you an idea if the company is overvalued or undervalued.

15. *Check your attitude towards investment.*
- You must invest with the right approach in a stock and not because the stock is bought by somebody you look up to or have faith in.
- Are you able to honestly evaluate the stock without the fear of incurring a loss when you have held it for too long?
- Are you trying to compete with others by picking up more stocks?
- Please see that you are not a victim of any psychological investment biases such as availability bias, gambler's fallacy, recency bias, confirmation bias, familiarity bias, representative bias, hindsight bias, consistency bias, commitment bias, disposition effect bias, etc.
- For checking the biases, answer the following questions:

  a. Is the stock held by a person I admire, which is why I want to invest? (Representative/Authority bias)
  b. Am I driven by recently published data, or have I looked at evidence of the past one or two decades? (Recency bias)

c. Am I relying on readily available information about the company, or have I dug deeper into unavailable details too? (Availability bias)

d. Have I checked any other well-doing company that failed despite looking equally promising? Have I tried to find out why it failed? (Confirmation bias)

e. Do I respond to negative news actively? (Consistency bias)

f. Am I willing to readily invite change in my investment portfolio? (Attachment bias)

Too often, you will have seen doctors following a checklist for surgery or pre-take-off checklists followed by aircraft staff for passengers' safety. Do you know that the strict norms of following a checklist have minimized surgical errors to a great extent? Moreover, the pilots can give you an error-free, smooth ride only because they follow a strict checklist before flying.

Such checklists are used everywhere to smoothen the operations processes. For example, checklists are used before software releases, for sports, academic research, professional driving lessons, and almost everywhere else.

Although stock market investment is not as critical as surgeries or flying an aircraft, having a checklist can help you stay focused and organised, and help minimize errors to a great extent.

In the words of American polymath and founding father of the United States Benjamin Franklin, 'An investment in knowledge pays the best interest.' So always be a learner on the go.

Conclusion

The stock market is like a life partner,
You love it, or you hate it,
You surely need it!

This book has been the prologue to the creation of your successful investment journey. Now, the reading ends, and the action begins!

I am sure that now you will get into stock investment with a confident, self-initiated approach rather than relying blindly on stock brokers or professional investment agencies.

This book indicates a paradigm shift in investment practices from long-standing traditional trading to the modern principles of value investing. The two essential takeaways from this book are: 'Slow and steady wins the race!' and 'You need to play this game with the right intent to win the game.' I hope this book acts as an eye-opener to solve the time-hallowed mystery of stock investment.

Although just by reading this book, you won't become an expert in stock investment right from the first day. But this book will surely act as a guide to help you chart out your investment course, which will help you create good wealth.

A significant chunk of the young population is actively investing in the stock market. The only intent in writing this book is to encourage every individual to invest in stocks in a well-informed manner, as it has the potential to generate an alternative source of income to sustain a good standard of living.

Thank you for sparing some of your precious time for *Investonomy*. If you enjoyed reading this book, do share it with your friends, family, and acquaintances to help them benefit too. Please feel free to share your feedback, ideas, and suggestions with me at support@finology.in.

Happy investing!

Here's a Pleasant Surprise for You!

FINOLOGY.IN®

TICKER

As I've mentioned throughout the course of this book, speculating is a disastrous strategy in the stock market. So, equity research should be an integral part of your journey to create wealth with stock market investing. I understand that it can be overwhelming at times, and it also takes substantial time and effort. But what if I tell you that you can get it done through a virtual assistant? Yes, that's true!

'Ticker' is the revolutionary equity research tool and stock screener that I'm referring to. There are other equity research tools out there that miss out on some feature or the other. Ticker has been developed to address this issue. Be it stock baskets prepared using proven strategies, a robust platform for stock analysis, or detailed peer comparison, Ticker has got you covered.

Experienced investors and newbie investors face different kinds of issues while investing. In fact, their ways of researching are also different, along with their research requirements. Ticker is a wholesome tool that helps all kinds of investors make the right decision, and more importantly, a well-informed decision.

ticker
By Finology

| Stock Analysis is Now Simple | |

FINOLOGY.IN®

Features

Get All the Information You Need
- Comprehensive Research Reports
- Credit Rating Reports
- Investor Presentations

Peer Comparison
Choose the Best in Industry with Better Accuracy
- Intricately Detailed Data
- Compare Three Companies at a Time
- Industry-Wise Suggested Parameters

Bundles
Get Started with Investment Strategies that Provide Better Customization
- Options to Suit Different Investing Styles
- Daily Updates Based on Market Behavior
- Robust Parameters Crafted by Experts

Smart Portfolio & Alerts
Build a Smarter Portfolio with Better Analysis
- Portfolio analysis through astute algorithms
- Visual representation of your investment style
- Intelligent alerts & notifications to keep you one step ahead!

Scan the QR Code to get there directly!

Acknowledgements

'Gratitude turns what we have into enough.'

This anonymous quote makes a lot of sense to me, especially after completing this book. I've tried including all the investing fundamentals, theories, principles, and technical knowledge that I've acquired through years of learning and implementation. The book wouldn't have been possible without the blessings of my parents and mentors and the contributions of numerous people who worked selflessly to make this happen.

The book has attained its final shape after rigorous editing and proofreading by Ratan Deep Singh and Chandni Agrawal. Enlightening technical inputs have been provided by Panjul Agrawal and Urvi Kotak. It would've been a slightly boring read without the creative images designed by Dev Vishwakarma and Mohit Malviya. Thank you, Priya Jain, for providing innovative inputs along with moral support for this book. Finally, I'd like to extend sincere gratitude towards Nitishiree Gupta for her contribution in preparing the draft of this book.